Joseph W. White

White's Guide to Florida and her Famous Resorts

Containing a Brief History of Florida; her Climate, Health, soil,

Agricultural...

Joseph W. White

White's Guide to Florida and her Famous Resorts

Containing a Brief History of Florida; her Climate, Health, soil, Agricultural...

ISBN/EAN: 9783744757249

Printed in Europe, USA, Canada, Australia, Japan

Cover: Foto ©ninafisch / pixelio.de

More available books at **www.hansebooks.com**

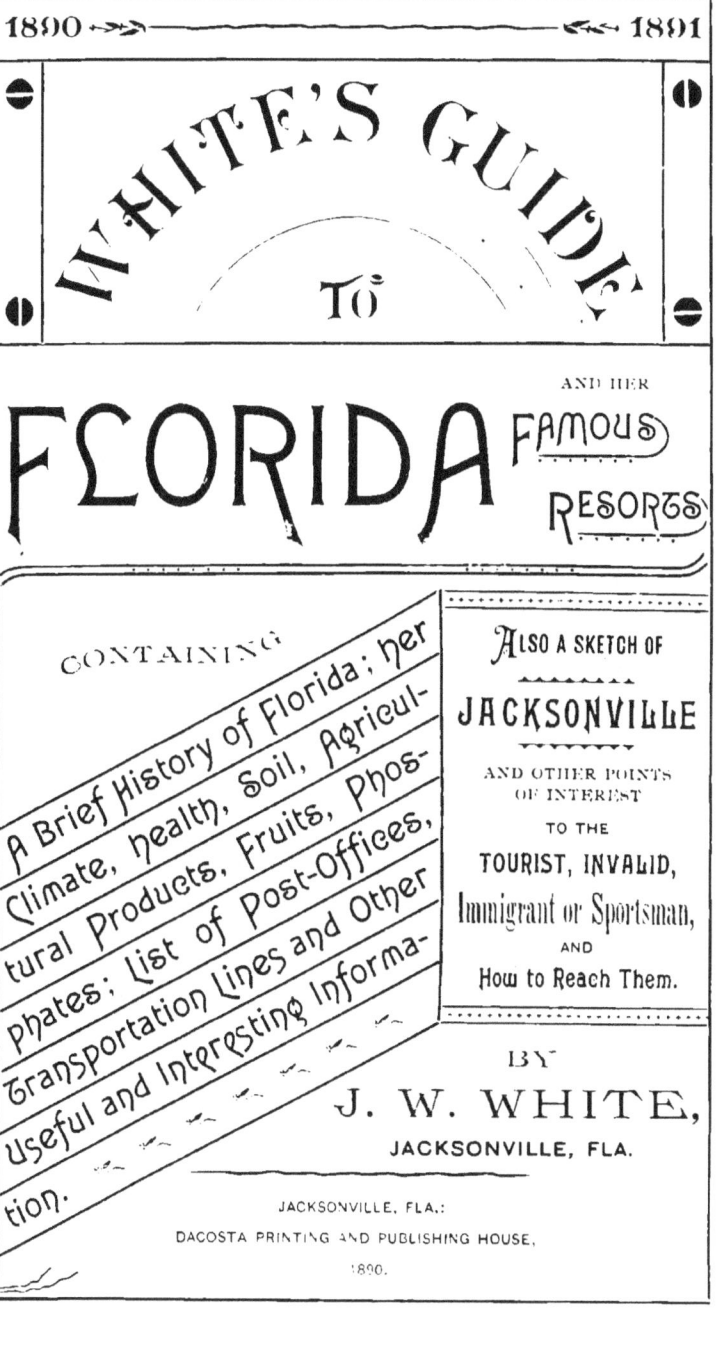

Introductory.

IN presenting this work to the public, we feel that those disposed to criticise may find an opportunity for the exercise of that universal talent. An effort has been made to avoid a mass of dry facts and figures, or a collection of elaborate statements which will not stand investigation. The historian and statistician were looking for a better country than Florida when the work was begun, and up to the time of going to press had not returned. What the writer has aimed at is the condensation of matter relative to Florida as the great sanitarium and orange grove of the world, which would suffice to fill volumes, and as there has been barely space to tell the truth in regard to the exciting history, the wonderful climate, rich soil, and boundless wealth of health and varied productions, as well as her remarkable progress, the following pages will be found worthy of confidence. For a like reason no attempt has been made to become enthusiastic, and the scenes described will be found to more than realize the accounts of their various attractions.

J. W. WHITE.

Florida.

WHERE earth is an Eden, the climate a balm;
Bright hues deck the fields, and aloft waves the palm;
O'er the hammocks its perfume the jasmine flings;
To the live-oak the solemn gray drapery clings;
Wide the cypress its vast leafy canopy throws;
And in loveliness blossoms the Florida Rose.

The great State of Florida is a region of not only wonderful possibilities, but great probabilities. In its mild, healthy and equable climate, exempt alike from the rigorous winters of the ice-bound North and the heated summers of less favored sections; in its boundless wealth of luscious fruits, agricultural products, lumber, phosphate, fish and other important productions, there is that which is real, solid, hopeful. Others have gone through the dark days of anxiety, and the thorns of pioneering are removed. The doubtful period is past, and the future beams forth like the sun in heaven. Among the thousands who have found homes of peace and plenty many have become rich, while all have been made content. Many thousands more will quickly follow the inspiration of such an alluring example. During the next twenty years Florida will be the theatre of many vast public enterprises. Fortunes will be made in every nook and corner, and in every industry, and thousands now living will yet acquire and enjoy the luxuries of wealth. Cities yet unborn will be built and populated where now are virgin forests. This has been the history of all the older sections of our Union. While recollecting that "history repeats itself," the restless reader, looking from his

Take the SAVANNAH, FLORIDA & WESTERN RAILWAY,
The Through Car and Short Line to and from Florida.

quiet home "back West or East" toward a new home should carefully ponder over a still more important fact; that is, that Florida is infinitely superior in climate and in all resources which go to make up great States and thrifty people to any region of similar extent on earth. Every new comer cannot gain fame and riches here, but he can gain a good livelihood, and will, all the time, have the consciousness of being identified with a region whose glories he can proudly proclaim at all times and in all lands.

There is but one Florida, and she offers to the tourist, invalid, immigrant or sportsman a balm which will lengthen life and enrich the fleeting hours.

It is the best inheritance bequeathed by the Father to His children; long reserved, but revealed at this day, possessing treasures such as none of her sister States possess or can secure.

Some would compare Florida with Italy. There can be no comparison, except by contrast. Italy is a region of hills and mountains, snow-capped during a part of the year. Florida is nearly a plain, and in most of it snow was never seen. Florida is a peninsula, and extends into the warmest portion of the ocean and on the border of the trade winds; its breezes are tempered by the genial equability of the Gulf stream.

Spain and the Grecian Isles compare with Italy as to climate and productions. Florida stands alone; no place can be compared to her. Her highest praise is to call her by *her own beautiful Castilian name*, FLORIDA! No country can be like Florida, and she needs no gems borrowed from another's crown.

Florida differs from all other countries and States; it differs from itself in regions and parallels, as if to supply the desires of all choosing to locate within its borders. In Florida may be found locations suited to the tastes and desires of every would-be resident, and every production the agriculturist may desire to grow.

Between twenty-five degrees and thirty-one degrees north latitude, and between eighty degrees and eighty-eight degrees west longitude from Greenwich lies the State of Florida, containing 58,680 square miles, 4,440 square miles being water surface, and the remaining 54,240 square miles land surface, or 34,713,600 acres.

The peninsular portion, measuring from the northern boundary, extends south about 400 miles, with an average width of about 100 miles. The northern part of the State extends from the Atlantic westward along the southern boundary of the States of

☞ Visit Green Cove Springs, a delightful Retreat for the Tourist, Invalid, Immigrant or Sportsman. Excellent Hotels, the Borden Parks, Fine Fishing and Hunting. Reached by Steamer or Train.

FLORIDA COAST SCENE.

Take the SAVANNAH, FLORIDA & WESTERN RAILWAY,
The Through Car and Short Line to and from Florida.

Georgia and Albama about 375 miles, with a width to the Gulf of from forty to ninety miles.

The average altitude of Florida, as set forth in Toner's Dictionary of Elevations, is sixty feet above the level of the sea. Louisiana, the next lowest, averages seventy-five feet above the level of the sea. The largest portion of the territory of all the States on the Atlantic coast from Maine to Florida is less than 300 feet above the sea level by this authority. Many are of the impression that high places are the most healthy, but this is not always true, and is not the testimony of experience in Florida. Sometimes the lower places in the same neighborhood have had quite the advantage in point of health. In the Old World some healthful and fertile localities are below the level of the sea, as the Valley of the Jordan, more than 1,000 feet below the surface of the Mediterranean Sea, the shores of the Caspian Sea; and portions of Holland have been reclaimed from the ocean by its dykes.

With a coast line of almost 1,200 miles, accessible with small boats all along the shore, the long, narrow peninsula of Florida puts its whole surface in near approach to the commerce of the ocean. A number of the best harbors of the United States are on the coast of Florida, and, with an equitable expenditure upon them, will have a larger number of ports accessible to ocean steamers than any other State. Nineteen of the rivers of Florida are already navigable by steamers to the distance, in the aggregate, of over 1,000 miles. These streams, in some instances, flowing entirely across the State, make transportation available to extensive areas, and, in almost every instance, have at their mouths such harbor facilities as make coastwise navigation to vessels of moderate draught safe and active.

HISTORY.

"Oh, Florida, romantic land,
Enraptured, I thy praises sing;
For Nature smiles on every hand,
And winter is as fair as spring."

THE history of Florida begins with its discovery by Juan Ponce de Leon, which dates as early as 1512. Its then unmolested shores were discovered on the 27th day of March by this adventurous navigator, who landed his craft on the 2d day of April following, near where the city of Fernandina now stands. There seems, however, to have been no attempt made to establish a settlement at that point at the time. Ponce

☞ Visit Green Cove Springs, a delightful Retreat for the Tourist, Invalid Immigrant or Sportsman. Excellent Hotels, the Borden Parks, Fine Fishing and Hunting. Reached by Steamer or Train.

de Leon was first made Governor of the territory by the Spanish government in the year 1521; yet there is no record of any noteworthy progress having been made until 1565, when Pedro Menendez sailed from Cadiz, Spain, on the 1st of July; arrived at

ON THE ST. JOHNS

St. Augustine Bay August 28th, and, on the 29th of the same month, founded the city of St. Augustine, which place is reputed to be by far the oldest town in the United States, being certainly the most ancient in Florida, and figuring the most prominently

Take the SAVANNAH, FLORIDA & WESTERN RAILWAY,
The Through Car and Short Line to and from Florida.

in the early history of the State. Other discoveries were made along the coast of Florida, at various points, subsequent to that made by Ponce de Leon, by other noted navigators whose names are familiar.

The early history of Florida was not one of rapid and encouraging development, as the progress of the colony during the successive territorial administrations was of but little consequence to the foreign powers under whose control the territory remained. The most important of the changes of ownership through which Florida has passed was that effected by the treaty of February 22, 1819, between John Quincy Adams, Secretary of State of the United States, and Louis de Onis, Envoy Extraordinary and Minister Plenipotentiary of the Kingdom of Spain, by which Spain ceded the Floridas, East and West, to the United States, the Territory being admitted into the Union in 1845. Spain controlled the territory from the discovery by Ponce de Leon up to the year 1763, at which time the Floridas, East and West, were ceded to Great Britain, Florida being subject to British authority until 1783. Great Britain, however, had lost her thirteen American colonies in the war of 1876, and her government receded the Floridas to Spain in 1783. Thus for more than 250 years Florida was in the grasp of powers indifferent to its welfare and progress, as they regarded it at too great a distance from their local interests to promise advantage from immigration and settlement.

From the time that Florida was admitted into the Union up to the present the increase in wealth and population has been truly wonderful, and it is safe to predict that the future will be full of heaven's richest blessings. The population of the State in 1830, and at the close of each decade since, was as follows:

```
1830. . . . . . . . . . . . . . . . . . . . .  37,730
1840. . . . . . . . . . . . . . . . . . . . .  54,477
1850. . . . . . . . . . . . . . . . . . . . .  87,445
1860. . . . . . . . . . . . . . . . . . . . . 140,424
1870. . . . . . . . . . . . . . . . . . . . . 187,748
1880. . . . . . . . . . . . . . . . . . . . . 269,490
```

And in 1890, with a careful count, would reach above 400,000; a fact which every citizen should feel justly proud of. The history of Florida has been full of progress, and the time is not far distant when Florida will hold the proud position she is destined to fill—the brightest star in the Union.

☞ Visit Green Cove Springs, a delightful Retreat for the Tourist, Invalid, Immigrant or Sportsman. Excellent Hotels, the Borden Parks, Fine Fishing and Hunting. Reached by Steamer or Train.

CLIMATE.

Knowest thou the land where the lemon trees bloom,
Where the gold orange grows in the green thickets' gloom,
Where the wind ever soft from the blue heaven blows,
And groves are of myrtle and orange and rose?

RETURNING FROM A DEER HUNT.

"FLORIDA has many attractions, but the crown and pearl of them all is her incomparable climate. So genial and balmy is it that in winter, as well as summer, even invalids can live an out-door life, breathe the pure, bracing air, and bask in the warm sunshine.

Take the SAVANNAH, FLORIDA & WESTERN RAILWAY,
The Through Car and Short Line to and from Florida.

Western Railway of Florida.

Lake Santa Fe Route.

The only Rail Line to Melrose and the Finest Lake Region of Florida.

Unexcelled Attractions for Tourist and Sportsman.

HUNTING AND FISHING
UNSURPASSED.

Melrose, situated on Lake Santa Fe, surrounded by beautiful clear water lakes and orange groves, is indisputably one of the healthiest places in the State.

THE NEW HOTEL SANTA FE,

Open Nov. 15 under popular management.

PARLOR CARS ON ALL TRAINS WITHOUT EXTRA CHARGE.

Direct connection at Green Cove Springs with the J. T. & K. W. Ry. and steamers on St. Johns River.

L. E. BARKER,
General Superintendent.

☛ Visit Green Cove Springs, a delightful Retreat for the Tourist, Invalid, Immigrant or Sportsman. Excellent Hotels, the Borden Parks, Fine Fishing and Hunting. Reached by Steamer or Train.

"It is difficult to give a definite idea of its beauty. Owing to the peninsular position of Florida, its climate is unique. It is unlike that of any other Southern State or Santa Barbara. You find nothing like it in Southern Europe or Algiers. This climate is altogether peculiar. There is nothing equal to it on the face of the earth." Of course, the climate is warm in the direct rays of the sun—hot, even; but it is scarcely ever sultry, muggy, prostrating. The sun, though hot, does not smite. Sunstrokes are almost unknown; I have never heard of one in the State. The reason is that the heat is marvelously tempered by the cool sea breezes which continually play across the peninsula. Even in the hottest part of the day step into the shade and at once you find the air deliciously cool and refreshing, and, at the same time, indescribably soft and balmy.

But some one may ask, "What of your Florida summers; are they not unbearable?" We most emphatically answer, "No!" for there are but few places on the face of the globe more delightful during the summer than Florida.

The only drawback to this season is its length, generally extending from May until October. During the summer just passed, when every paper from the North gave long lists of fatal cases of sunstroke and prostration from heat, in the whole of Florida there was not one case reported, either fatal or otherwise. The average height of the thermometer at noon is less than eighty-six degrees, and even this is so tempered by the constant sea breeze that it is more endurable at that rate than would be a much lower temperature in the North.

Many will be disposed to doubt this, but when they consider our location on this narrow strip of rolling land, surrounded on three sides by miles and miles of water, from off which blow the cooling breezes, and also the fact that nearly every day during the "rainy season," extending from June to September, we are favored with rains that lower the temperature perceptibly, they must admit that our location is very favorable for making our summers pleasant. The sun shines brightly, and, of course, it is warm in its rays. Still we have known people to come here from the extreme northern portion of the Union and work every day in the sun without experiencing any evil effects. One great advantage that the summers have over that of other sections is our cool nights. Immediately after sunset a cool east breeze commences, and generally continues through the night; and, almost without exception, covering is in demand and comfortable before morning. Inhabitants of northern countries, where the hot, sul-

Take the SAVANNAH, FLORIDA & WESTERN RAILWAY,
The Through Car and Short Line to and from Florida.

A. E. G. BETT & CO.,

Successors to E. E. HOOKER & CO.,

Florida Coffee & Spice Mills.

WHOLESALE AND RETAIL DEALERS IN

Teas, Coffees, Spices,
Baking Powder, Extracts,
Bluing, Pearline,
Paper and Paper Bags,
Butter Trays, Twine, etc., etc.

28 OCEAN STREET,

Jacksonville, Florida.

JOHN O'NEIL,
MANUFACTURER AND DEALER IN

Rough & Planed Lumber, Mouldings, Brackets

All kinds of Scrolled Sawing and Turned Work, Rived and Sawed Cypress Shingles, Fencing, Laths, Fruit and Vegetable Crates, Etc.

All Orders Filled with Promptness and Dispatch.

O. L. KEENE,

Millinery, Dress Goods, Trimmings, Notions,

Laces, Kid Gloves, Parasols, Silk Umbrellas, Zephyrs, and all Material for Fancy Work.

No. 59 West Bay Street, corner of Laura.
JACKSONVILLE, FLA.

☞ Visit Green Cove Springs, a delightful Retreat for the Tourist, Invalid, Immigrant or Sportsman. Excellent Hotels, the Borden Parks, Fine Fishing and Hunting. Reached by Steamer and Train.

try nights, following the broiling-hot days, make sleep and rest almost impossible, will know how to appreciate our Florida summer nights when once they have given them a trial.

It is very difficult for denizens of the North to believe that our Florida summers are else but intolerable, and, for the especial benefit of these doubting Thomases, we furnish the following comparative table of the temperature of the different States. By reference to this it will be seen that ours is the most equable climate on the American continent:

STATE OR TERRITORY.	DEGREES.		
	Minimum	Maximum	Difference
Florida	105	10	95
Louisiana	105	0	105
Mississippi	105	— 05	110
Alabama	105	— 10	115
West Virginia	100	— 20	120
Georgia	105	— 20	125
Ohio	105	— 25	130
Kansas	110	— 20	130
Connecticut	105	— 30	135
Oregon	110	— 25	135
Illinois	105	— 35	140
Nebraska	110	— 30	140
New York	105	— 35	140
Idaho	115	— 30	145
Colorado	110	— 45	155
Dakota	110	— 45	155
California	115	— 45	160
Montana	115	— 50	165

Much more might be said of our climate, but space forbids. We can only add, come and see.

HEALTH.

*"And the pale health-seeker findeth there
The wine of life in its pleasant air."*

HEALTH is the chief aim of humanity, or, at least, it should be, for without it all of the favors lavished upon our devoted heads by Dame Nature amount to naught; they are fleeting and transitory, and are banished by the first appearance of the demon of ill health. You may be surrounded

Take the SAVANNAH, FLORIDA & WESTERN RAILWAY,
The Through Car and Short Line to and from Florida.

MERRILL-STEVENS ENGINEERING CO.,

A. D. STEVENS. J. EUGENE MERRILL. A. R. MERRILL.

Mechanical and Electrical Engineers.

IRON AND STEEL FORGING, BOILER MAKING.

Boilers and Engines, Phosphate Dredging, Mining and Drying Machinery.

MARINE WORK A SPECIALTY.

Workmen Sent to Any Part of the State.

SECOND-HAND MACHINERY BOUGHT  SOLD.

WRITE FOR ESTIMATES AND PRICES.

Office and Shops: 138 & 140 E. Bay Street,
JACKSONVILLE, FLA.

☞ Visit Green Cove Springs, a delightful Retreat for the Tourist, Invalid, Immigrant or Sportsman. Excellent Hotels, the Borden Parks, Fine Fishing and Hunting. Reached by Steamer or Train.

by all mundane luxuries, and imagine yourself in the seventh heaven of happiness, when the stinging pangs of rheumatism, the choking hand of asthma, or the dread reflection that your chief heritage on earth is a pulmonary disease, comes to you and banishes pleasure as rapidly as our Florida sunshine and resinous breezes banish the pallor from the cheeks of the "puny" and paint them with the roseate hue of health.

MOONLIGHT ON THE LAKES.

This, then, is the chief point to be considered when you contemplate a removal from your land of ice and snow to one of perpetual sunshine and summer—

"To a land by orange blossoms shaded,
 Where summer ever lingers on the air."

Do not think, however, that our climate is only healthy because it is warm, or that all warm climates are healthy, for they, most emphatically, are not. But when you find a place where sudden changes of the temperature are rarely known, where there is no stagnant water and decaying vegetation to breed malarial diseases, where the land is high and dry and swept continually by ocean winds, you may be satisfied that you have found a healthy location, and make your plans accordingly.

People in the last stages of that most flattering of all diseases —consumption—are prone to be hopeful, and annually many of

Take the SAVANNAH, FLORIDA & WESTERN RAILWAY,
The Through Car and Short Line to and from Florida.

Kornahrens' Steam Bottling Works.

—AGENT FOR—

F. W. Cook Brewing Company's Beer,

AND MANUFACTURER OF

SODA WATER, SARSAPARILLA, GINGER ALE, SELTZER, AND SYRUPS OF ALL KINDS,

AND DEALER IN
BOTTLED BEER IN PINTS AND HALF PINTS.

72 EAST BAY ST., Meyer & Muller Block,   JACKSONVILLE, FLA.

L. O. BECKER,
THE TAILOR,

BURBRIDGE BLOCK.   MAIN (PINE) STREET.

Jacksonville, Florida.

FINEST WORK.   LOWEST PRICES.   LATEST STYLES.
EVERYTHING AS REPRESENTED.

T. MURPHY,
Iron and Brass Founder and Machinist.

ENGINES, SAW MILLS, PUMPS AND MACHINERY IN GENERAL REPAIRED AT SHORT NOTICE.
Iron and Brass Castings Made to Order.

136 East Bay Street, JACKSONVILLE, FLA.

☞ Visit Green Cove Springs, a delightful Retreat for the Tourist, Invalid, Immigrant, or Sportsman. Excellent Hotels, the Borden Parks, Fine Fishing and Hunting. Reached by Steamer or Train.

them come tottering Floridaward. Alas! they come to stay, and the sad soughing of the wind through the stately pines above their graves sighs a warning to others, which they should heed. If you are in the last stages of consumption stay at home, wherever that home may be, where, surrounded by friends and loved ones, the last days of your life may be made comfortable, and you can die in peace, with a loving hand to close your eyes in that last, long sleep. Florida will not cure you—nothing will. So stay at home and die among friends. There are exceptions, however, even to this rule. In some cases of consumption, where hemorrhages are rapidly drawing the sufferer to an untimely grave, we have known remarkable cures to be effected in a short time. The healing air of our peninsula appeared to give new life to the wasted lungs and cause them to heal, and, to all appearances, become as sound as ever.

So much, then, for those who have allowed this dread disease to run so long, and get so firm a hold upon them. Now a word to those who are troubled with weak lungs and are liable to go into consumption at any moment, and we will leave this sad, though important, subject for one more cheerful. To those who fear consumption, or lung trouble in any form, we say come to Florida, and come at once. Do not delay a day, or you may be in the lamentable condition of those unfortunate creatures above mentioned. Come while you are young and have the vitality to fight off the disease; come 'ere your frame is emaciated by the dread scourge, and grim death stares you in the face. Here you will find in our salubrious climate, in our healing air and our life-inspiring sunshine, the panacea for all your ills.

The climate of our State, however, is not only beneficial to weak lungs, but is also highly recommended by eminent medical authorities for bronchial, throat troubles and asthma.

The healthfulness of no locality averts the divinely indicated limitation placed upon human life as "three score and ten." Sanitary science attaches paramount importance to conditions or environments as preservative from many avoidable disease, thereby increasing the sum total of human happiness, as well as aiding greatly in prolonging life.

The interest taken in these favorable conditions is no longer confined to the few who devote themselves to the critical investigation as to the laws governing health, but the masses are deeply interested in ascertaining the sanitary requisites at home, and if they contemplate a change of abode desire that it shall be a land

Take the SAVANNAH, FLORIDA & WESTERN RAILWAY,
The Through Car and Short Line to and from Florida.

NEW STORE. NEW GOODS.

F. A. PELLERIN,

149 WEST BAY STREET,

FURNITURE,

HOUSE FURNISHINGS,

BEDDING AND STOVES,

PICTURES, MATTING, BABY CARRIAGES,

And, in fact, everything usually to be found in a first-class Furniture Store.

WINDOW SHADES A SPECIALTY.

LATEST STYLES. LOWEST PRICES.

WILLIAM BUCKLER,

FLORIDA MONUMENTAL,

MARBLE, GRANITE,

AND

SCULPTOR WORKS,

MAIN STREET, JACKSONVILLE, FLA.

Being a practical marble dealer, I deem it a duty to inform my friends and the public generally that those who desire to erect Monuments should exercise the utmost care in selecting the grade of Marble. My work is of the highest order of style and workmanship; and remember I use none of the cheap grades of marble, but the best, and work at the lowest prices.

☞ Visit Green Cove Springs, a delightful Retreat for the Tourist, Invalid, Immigrant or Sportsman. Excellent Hotels, the Borden Parks, Fine Fishing and Hunting. Reached by Steamer or Train.

not only "flowing with milk and honey," but also that it shall be eminently calculated to preserve them from the ills of life.

Poverty's most efficient ally is disease. There is a world of comfort in Richardson's proverb: "National health is national wealth."

Surgeon-General Lawton, of the United States Army, in an official report written before the war, presents the advantages of the Peninsular State at large.

WAKULLA SPRINGS, FLA. (ON THE F. C. & P. R. R.)

Perhaps the freedom from suspicious bias, which is properly attached to much that is written of the booming nature, will secure it a credence that its authority deserves.

"The climate of Florida is remarkably agreeable, being subject to fewer atmospheric variations, and its thermometer ranges much less than that of any other part of the United States, except a portion of the coast of California. For example, the winter at Fort Snelling, Minnesota, is forty-eight degrees colder than

Take the SAVANNAH, FLORIDA & WESTERN RAILWAY,
The Through Car and Short Line to and from Florida.

A. J. WALKER,

Corner Bay and Bridge Sts.,

WHOLESALE AND RETAIL DEALER IN

FOREIGN AND DOMESTIC

CIGARS AND TOBACCO

CHEWING TOBACCOS A SPECIALTY.

Full Line of Oranges and Fine Fruits in their Season.
CONFECTIONERY, NUTS, ETC.

W. JEACLE & CO.,

GENTLEMEN'S FASHIONABLE

BOOT AND SHOE MAKERS,

L'ENGLE BLOCK,

CORNER PINE AND ADAMS STS.

The Davis Gallery,

13 1-2 WEST BAY ST.

You will find it the best equipped Studio in the South, while the work turned out by far excells any done in this State, both for style, pose and finish. Never in the history of this Gallery has the work reached such an artistic standpoint as it has under its present management.

☞ Visit Green Cove Springs, a delightful Retreat for the Tourist, Invalid Immigrant or Sportsman. Excellent Hotels, the Borden Parks, Fine Fishing and Hunting. Reached by Steamer or Train.

at Fort Brook, Florida; but the summer at Fort Brook, Florida, is only eight degrees warmer. The mean annual temperature of Augusta, Georgia, is nearly eight degrees, and that of Fort Gibson, Arkansas, upwards of ten degrees lower than at Tampa, yet in both these places the mean summer temperature is higher than at Fort Brook, Tampa Bay. In the summer season the mercury rises higher in every part of the United States, and even in Canada, than it does along the coast of Florida. This is shown by meteorological statistics in this bureau.

"As respects health, the climate of Florida stands pre-eminent. That the peninsular climate of Florida is much more salubrious than that of any other State in the Union is clearly established by the medical statistics of the army. Indeed, the statistics in this bureau demonstrate the fact that diseases that result from malaria are of a much milder type in the peninsula of Florida than in any other State in the Union. These records show that the ratio of deaths to the number of cases of remittent fever has been much less than among the troops serving in any other portion of the United States.

"In the Middle Division of the United States the proportion is one death to thirty-six cases of remitting fever; in the Northern Division, one to fifty-two; in the Southern Division, one to fifty-four; in Texas, one to seventy-eight; in California, one to one hundred and twenty-two; in New Mexico, one to one hundred and forty-eight; while in Florida it is but *one to two hundred and eighty-seven.*"

According to the statistics prepared by United States Surgeon-General Hammond Florida is the healthiest State in the Union. He shows the death rate in Florida to be one in 1,447; in Massachusetts, one in 254; in New York, one in 473; and in Minnesota, one in 755.

SOIL.

THERE is no soil susceptible of greater improvement, at equal expense, in the universe. It is exceedingly diversified, and its varied character is suited not only to the crops of other States, generally, but, because of its near approach to a tropical climate, to some products not grown elsewhere in the States. The soil is classed as first, second and third rate pine lands, and as high and low hammocks and swamp lands.

The pine lands cover much the larger portion of the State, and travelers in the train, or over the highways through them,

Take the SAVANNAH, FLORIDA & WESTERN RAILWAY,
The Through Car and Short Line to and from Florida.

LOOK HERE!
M. A. DOWLING,
CORNER ADAMS AND BRIDGE STS.,
Will Sell you at Lowest Prices
FANCY AND STAPLE GROCERIES,
FRESH MEATS AND VEGETABLES,
Fine Cigars and Tobacco,
EGGS AND POULTRY A SPECIALTY.
FISH AND OYSTERS IN THEIR SEASON.
Free Delivery to Any Part of the City.
REMEMBER THE PLACE,
Cor. Adams and Bridge Sts., Jacksonville, Fla.

W. P. SUMNER,
Wholesale Dealer in
FINE BUTTER AND CHEESE,
GROCERIES,
54 W. Bay Street, Jacksonville, Fla.

AGENT FOR
Elgin Condensed Milk, York State and Elgin Butter, York State and Sheboygan Cheese.

☞ Visit Green Cove Springs, a delightful Retreat for the Tourist, Invalid, Immigrant or Sportsman. Excellent Hotels, the Borden Parks, Fine Fishing and Hunting. Reached by Steamer or Train.

are not apt to be impressed, in such casual inspection with their real worth. The white sand on the immediate surface is taken as conclusive testimony against them; but that is not all sand which, in the careless glance, appears to be. In a large portion of the State this sand is mixed with finely comminuted bits of shells or carbonate of lime.

The second-class pine lands, which have been adjudged by competent authority to be in the largest proportion, are all pro-

ORANGE GROVE (ON THE F. C. & P. R. R.).

ductive. They are not hilly, but, for the most part, undulating in their surface. Some of the sand hills of Hernando County are regarded among the highest points in the State. Underlying the surface is clay, marl, lime-rock and sand. These lands, from their accessibility and productiveness, the facility of fertilizing with cattle, and the impression of their healthfulness above hammock lands, have induced their enclosure and tillage, when the richer hammock lands were near by, but more difficult to prepare for cultivation.

Take the SAVANNAH, FLORIDA & WESTERN RAILWAY,
The Through Car and Short Line to and from Florida.

Are You Going to Paper?
IF SO, GO TO
ROBINSON'S,

15 W. Bay St., Jacksonville, Fla., and
45 Charlotte St., St. Augustine,

AND SEE HIS LARGE NEW STOCK OF
WALL PAPER,
ROOM MOULDINGS,
CORNICE POLES, WINDOW SHADES, ETC.
SEND FOR SAMPLES AND PRICES.
First-Class Work Guaranteed, and Prices Lower
than anywhere else in the State.

HEADQUARTERS
FOR
Wines, Liquors & Beers,
IMPORTED AND DOMESTIC.

JUG TRADE SOLICITED.
Special Attention given to all Mail Orders.

A. K. LEON,
18 WEST BAY ST., JACKSONVILLE, FLORIDA.
TELEPHONE 297.

☞ Visit Green Cove Springs, a delightful Retreat for the Tourist, Invalid, Immigrant or Sportsman. Excellent Hotels, the Borden Parks, Fine Fishing and Hunting. Reached by Steamer or Train.

FLORIDA'S AGRICULTURAL PRODUCTS.

January: Plant Irish potatoes,
Cabbage, peas, egg plants, tomatoes.

February: Fruits and vines,
Onions, melons, and grapes for wines.

March: Corn, oats and fine spring wheat.
And all that man or beast can eat.

April: Millet and lady peas;
Dig Irish potatoes and hive your bees.

May: Plant pepper and finger-tips,
And lay for sweet potato slips.

June: Once more turn up the ground,
And sow and reap, an endless round

July: Trees may now be set,
The soil, from kindly rains, is wet.

August: Harvest, one and all!
Sow turnips and cauliflowers for fall.

September: Spring is here again;
Now put your winter garden in.

October: 'Neath this genial sky
Sow oats and barley, wheat and rye.

November: Plant as heretofore,
Sow and reap, still more and more.

December: Ditch, manure and drain,
For lo! sweet spring is here again.

THOSE who have never carefully considered the statistics of the State have but little idea of what the State produces annually.

A large amount of long and short staple cotton is grown, both of which do well here, especially the former.

The sugar industry is being awakened, and considerable capital is being invested in machinery for its manufacture. The reclaimed lands of the State are well adapted to raising cane. At present it is grown all over the State for domestic purposes, each farmer having his own mill and evaporator, and making his own syrup and sugar, besides some for sale. Sugar cane grows better in Florida than anywhere else in the United States, the canes often growing twelve feet high, while in Louisiana they rarely grow over five feet.

Corn is the greatest cereal crop of Florida, and some of our farmers produce as many as from 2,000 to 4,000 bushels annually, and at the rate of from twelve to sixty bushels per acre.

Take the **SAVANNAH, FLORIDA & WESTERN RAILWAY,**
The Through Car and Short Line to and from Florida.

Dr. Geo. C. Mathews,

Physician and Surgeon,

OFFICE HOURS:
12 TO 1, 2 TO 4, 7 TO 8 P. M.

46 WEST DUVAL STREET

TELEPHONE 215

J. A. DOHM.   G. L. DOHM.

DOHM BRO'S,
CITY MARKET,
WHOLESALE AND RETAIL DEALERS IN
New York and Chicago Meats.
ALSO
STATE AGENTS FOR
NELSON, MORRIS & CO.,
CHICAGO.

P. O. Box 44.   Telephone 218.

JACKSONVILLE, FLA.

☞ Visit Green Cove Springs, a delightful Retreat for the Tourist, Invalid, Immigrant or Sportsman. Excellent Hotels, the Borden Parks, Fine Fishing and Hunting. Reached by Steamer and Train.

The planting of upland rice is increasing from year to year, and, with the introduction of improved machinery for cleaning it, it is fast becoming one of our staple crops, as it not only furnishes

COTTON FIELD NEAR TALLAHASSEE.

a salable article, but is a good grain for stock and poultry, containing more nutriment than oats.

Take the SAVANNAH, FLORIDA & WESTERN RAILWAY,
The Through Car and Short Line to and from Florida.

O. T. JONES,

COMMERCIAL

JOB * PRINTER.

FIRST-CLASS WORK.
LOW PRICES.   FULL COUNT.
CALL FOR ESTIMATES.

No. 8 East Bay St., JACKSONVILLE, FLA.

M. E. MATTOX,
(OAKLAND) JACKSONVILLE,
——DEALER IN——

Staple : and : Fancy : Groceries,
AT LOWEST PRICES.

PROMPT AND POLITE ATTENTION TO BUSINESS.

THE ONLY EXCLUSIVE
TRUNK FACTORY
IN THE STATE.

Genuine Alligator Satchels, Sole Leather Trunks,
LEATHER GOODS.
The Largest Stock and Finest Assortment.
Trunk Repairing a Specialty.
63 WEST BAY STREET,   JACKSONVILLE, FLORIDA.
WALKER, Manager.

☞ Visit Green Cove Springs, a delightful Retreat for the Tourist, Invalid, Immigrant or Sportsman. Excellent Hotels, the Borden Parks, Fine Fishing and Hunting. Reached by Steamer or Train.

Oats and rye are planted in the fall for winter pasture and harvested in the spring.

The growing of tobacco has lately become one of Florida's industries. Before the war Gadsden and adjoining counties produced some of the finest tobacco grown, and it was largely exported. Its planting has again been revived, and the quality of tobacco grown in the past year equals the best Cuban production.

Sweet potatoes can be grown anywhere in the State, and frequently attain the weight of ten to eighteen pounds, and produce from 100 to 500 bushels per acre, according to fertility of soil and cultivation.

Irish potatoes are grown for Northern markets, and bring from $5 to $8 per barrel. The home market is a good one, also, as they come to maturity at the time when Northern potatoes are out.

Peanuts are raised to a considerable extent in West Florida, but chiefly for home consumption and for fattening pork, which gives the meat a very delicious flavor.

Watermelons are at home in Florida, and grow to a perfection seldom attained in any other State. They produce well on new land, and often grow to weigh sixty pounds. A melon under twenty pounds is not considered worth handling for shipping.

Onion growing in Florida is increasing every year, and, as the result is quite satisfactory where they receive the proper cultivation, those who raised a small patch last year have trebled the quantity of seed planted. They require a rich and moist soil, and those who furnish this and give the proper cultivation are the ones who realize a handsome profit. The crop last year at no time brought less than $2 per bushel, and frequently more.

Cabbage is being cultivated to a great extent for shipping, as well as a number of other kinds of vegetables.

Nearly all kinds of vegetables do well, and find a ready sale at good prices, not only at home, but in the North, as they can be grown here when more northern climes are covered with ice and snow.

It may not be generally known that the agricultural products, *per capita*, of Florida double those of the average of all other Southern States.

This may seem strange to those who are ignorant of the truth, but we have taken pains to investigate the value of the

---

Take the SAVANNAH, FLORIDA & WESTERN RAILWAY,
The Through Car and Short Line to and from Florida.

WILLIAM FAIRLIE,
Successor to J. M. Fairlie & Bro.,
DRUGGIST AND PHARMACIST,
GENERAL DEALER IN

Drugs, Chemicals, Patent and Family Medicines, Proprietary Articles, Perfumery and Toilet Requisites, also Horse and Cattle Medicines,

GARDEN SEEDS, &C.

A large assortment of Paints, Oils, Varnishes, Brushes and other Painters' Supplies.

CHOICE STOCK OF TOBACCO AND CIGARS.

Empire One-Spoon Baking Powders in assorted sizes. Concentrated Essences and Flavoring Extracts, all flavors.

Grocers and others supplied at lowest wholesale prices. All orders will receive prompt and careful attention. Correspondence solicited. Address,

WILLIAM FAIRLIE,
JACKSONVILLE, FLA.

The Florida Times-Union,

DAILY AND WEEKLY.

DAILY,	. .	One Month, $1.00	SUNDAY, ...	Six Months,	$1.00
DAILY,	. . .	Three Months, 2.50	SUNDAY, ...	One Year,	2.00
DAILY,	. . .	Six Months, 5.00	WEEKLY, . . .	Six Months,	.50
DAILY, .		One Year, 10.00	WEEKLY, ...	One Year,	1.00

ADVERTISING RATES.

Advertising rates depend on Place in the Paper, and will be furnished on application.

Jacksonville, Fla.

☞ Visit Green Cove Springs, a delightful Retreat for the Tourist, Invalid, Immigrant, or Sportsman. Excellent Hotels, the Borden Parks, Fine Fishing and Hunting. Reached by Steamer or Train.

agricultural products of the other Southern States, and find it about $50, while our own is $100. With all California's wealth, her agricultural average is only $88; that of Tennessee only $33.25; Arkansas, $75; Mississippi, $73; Georgia, $50; and Alabama, $66.50. This is an exhibit which should make the pulse of every Floridian throb fast.

Below we reproduce the

MARKETABLE PRODUCTS OF FLORIDA—1889.

Roses and perfumes . . . . $	19,500
Limes and grape fruit	38,000
Poultry and eggs	235,000
Peaches and pears	160,500
Cow peas and fodder	185,750
Bees and honey	27,500
Arrow root	26,250
Hogs	165,000
Sheep (114,600 sheep)	152,500
Alligator hides and teeth	37,250
Strawberries	375,000
Milk and butter	165,000
Pineapples, cocoanuts, guavas, etc	47,500
Pinders	150,000
Grapes and wine	75,000
Wagons, buggies, etc	62,500
Ice	75,000
Hides and tallow	45,500
Nursery trees and shrubs	650,570
Brick, tile and chimneys	275,000
Artificial stone, etc	25,000
Moss	250,000
Sponges	750,000
Vegetables	1,150,000
Fish, oysters and turtles	375,000
Ships, boats, etc	140,000
Horses and mules	250,000
Sugar and molasses	800,000
Firewood	475,000
Rice	175,000
Railroad cars and repairing	300,000
Engines and boilers	45,000
Cotton seed	265,000
Cedar	500,000
Naval stores	825,000
Cattle	1,625,000

Take the SAVANNAH, FLORIDA & WESTERN RAILWAY,
The Through Car and Short Line to and from Florida.

NOTICE!!
SPECIAL!!! ATTENTION!!!

FREE EXCURSION
OVER
The O. K. and X. C. L. N. T. Route.

O. I. KETCHUM,
Gen ral Passenger Agent.

OFFICE, 310 BRIDGE STREET.

TICKETS GOOD ON ALL THIS COMPANY'S LINES.

CALL AT

310 BRIDGE ST.,

And Receive Free Ticket. Remember the Number.

While waiting for Ticket don't fail to examine my

IMMENSE STOCK OF
Furniture, Mattresses, Springs,
Comforters, Window Shades,
Blankets, Stoves, Etc., Etc.

!! SPECIAL !! !! ATTENTION !! is given to the Weekly and Monthly Payment plan of purchasing goods. I guarantee prices the cheapest in the city. I employ no canvassers or solicitors, thus giving you the benefit of the percentage paid by others who do business through so-called agents. Guaranteeing qualities the finest and styles the latest, I solicit a share of your patronage at the

GREAT BARGAIN HOUSE,
310 and 312 BRIDGE STREET.
FRANK W. R. HINMAN.

☞ Visit Green Cove Springs, a delightful Retreat for the Tourist, Invalid, Immigrant or Sportsman. Excellent Hotels, the Borden Parks, Fine Fishing and Hunting. Reached by Rail or Steamer.

Oranges and lemons	3,000,000
Cigars and manufactured tobacco	8,000,000
Corn, oats, hay, barley, rye, etc.	3,000,000
Sweet potatoes	1,000,000
Ducks and geese	10,000
Goats	15,000
Manufactured iron	32,000
Strawberry plants	32,000
Blackberries and other small fruits	25,000
Home-made fertilizers	275,000
Books, pamphlets, etc.	55,000
Railroad sleepers	450,000
Palmetto fibre	19,000
Lime	75,000
Leaf tobacco (2,137,900 pounds)	425,000
Furniture and mattrasses	85,000
Orange boxes and vegetable crates	235,000
Manufactured clothing	275,000
Shoes, etc.	40,000
Florida curiosities	45,000
Lathes and shingles	595,000
Piling timber	32,000
Fence rails	390,000
Cabbage and tomato plants	25,000
Tinware and sheetiron	45,000
Manufactured copper	5,000
Stone for building and cribbing	30,000
Harness, saddles, etc.	25,000
Birds, feathers, etc.	20,000
Poppy	9,500
Sawed lumber and timber	13,750,000
Other products	500,000
Total products	$44,436,820

It will be seen by the above that Florida has a greater producing capacity than she is given credit for; but, dear reader, do not imagine for a moment that you can settle in any part of the State and raise the whole list; that you can have the Alligator and LeConte pear growing side by side; that you can grow the sugar apple and peach together in any part of the State, for it cannot be done. It has not been our aim to tell where and how each could be raised, for it would require hundreds of pages to tell the interesting story.

Take the SAVANNAH, FLORIDA & WESTERN RAILWAY,
The Through Car and Short Line to and from Florida.

TRUMPELLER,
THE LEADING
Merchant Tailor,

AND DEALER IN

FIRST-CLASS READY-MADE CLOTHING,

Nos. 61 and 175 West Bay Street,

JACKSONVILLE, FLA.

READ THIS TWICE.

PHILIP KURTZ,
15 WEST BAY STREET,

Has the Largest and Best Assortment of Cigars, Tobacco and Smokers' Articles to be found in the State, Wholesale and Retail.

Sole Owner of Celebrated Whiskey Plug Tobacco.

PRICES ALWAYS THE LOWEST.

Iron ✧ and ✧ Wire ✧ Fencing.

LARGE VARIETY and LOW PRICES,

AT

W. BUCKLER'S

Florida Monumental, Marble, Granite and Sculptor Works.

MAIN STREET,   JACKSONVILLE, FLA.

☞ Visit Green Cove Springs, a delightful Retreat for the Tourist, Invalid, Immigrant or Sportsman. Excellent Hotels, the Borden Parks, Fine Fishing and Hunting. Reached by Rail or Steamer.

TOBACCO.

About the year 1565 Sir John Hawkins carried tobacco from Florida to England, and it is interesting to note what an important factor tobacco has been in the commerce of the world. Though an article of luxury, it was in the early history of Florida looked upon as a convenient medium of exchange. In 1620, while there was an abundance of tobacco in the colonies, there was a great scarity of females. An enterprising trader brought ninety young women from England to America and exchanged to the planters at 120 weight of female for 150 pounds of tobacco. King James issued a proclamation restraining this unlawful and obnoxious traffic. In 1570 Florida tobacco was first taken to Holland, and not until 1616 did the colonists of Virginia begin the planting of tobacco, the seed being obtained from what was then known as the Spanish Possessions—Florida.

Prior to the war Florida was celebrated for its tobacco, which was extensively and successfully cultivated. Recently the industry has been revived under the most favorable auspices, and promises to prove even more productive of wealth than in the past. The eyes of the world are now attracted to this region, which has again become famous for the large yield and very superior quality of its tobacco. The leaf grown here closely resembles, in appearance and flavor, the finest Havana wrappers, and we challenge any expert to detect the same, and is confessedly superior to that grown in any other part of the United States.

Fillers grown from genuine Vuelta Abajo seed, primes; price, one dollar per pound; fine quality, superior to medium Vuelta Abajo seed, seconds, seventy-five cents per pound, and will produce from 1,000 to 1,500 pounds per acre

The following extracts are taken from a "Report Upon the Cultivation of Tobacco in Florida," issued by Mr. H. R. Duval, Receiver of the Florida Railway and Navigation Company. It was made by experts, who visited the plantations in person, and may be relied upon as trustworthy and conservative:

"We have found tobacco growing on quite a variety of soil, but mainly on sandy loam, with red clay subsoil eight to ten inches deep; again on sandy loam with no subsoil, and, in some instances on newly cleared bottom or 'hummock' land, which seemed to be very rich, and required no fertilizer. The crop seems to flourish and do well on all these soils, but it appears to us that the tobacco grown on the 'hummock' land is of the best character, while its growth is more luxuriant. The country is well watered and timbered, and very fertile.

Take the SAVANNAH, FLORIDA & WESTERN RAILWAY,
The Through Car and Short Line to and from Florida.

W. B. CLARKSON, President.   W. P. WEBSTER, Vice-Pres.   E. I. ROBINSON, Treasurer.

THE DIME SAVINGS BANK
OF FLORIDA.
CHARTERED BY THE STATE.

Pays Four Per Cent. on Deposits. Authorized to Transact a General Banking Business.

Special Facilities for making and negotiating Loans on Real Estate and Collateral Security.

Receives Deposits from 10 cents upward, subject to Check.

BANK HOURS 10 A. M. TO 4 P. M. OPEN SATURDAY AND MONDAY EVENINGS FROM 6 TO 8.30 P. M.

Office, 76 **WEST FORSYTH STREET,**

OPPOSITE PUBLIC BUILDING SITE.

WANKLYN & CO.,

WHOLESALE AND RETAIL

Liquor Dealers,

91 WEST BAY STREET,

JACKSONVILLE, FLA.

☞ Visit Green Cove Springs, a delightful Retreat for the Tourist, Invalid, Immigrant or Sportsman. Excellent Hotels, the Borden Parks, Fine Fishing and Hunting. Reached by Steamer or Train.

"The climate of Florida is so favorable to the cultivation of tobacco that, aside from the first or original crop, two sucker crops can be raised. This is accomplished by cutting the stock off near the ground and leaving a sucker or shoot on the root, which will in a short time grow into a healthy, well developed stalk, on which the leaves will be lighter in weight, but larger and finer than the first crop. This, we believe, is an advantage enjoyed in no other tobacco-producing State in this country, as late springs and early frosts in the fall render a second or third crop in other sections an impossibility.

"With proper methods of growing, and careful, intelligent curing and sorting, we see no good reason why Florida should not only regain her former prestige as a tobacco-producing State, but, indeed, become the *leading* tobacco State; for the natural advantage she enjoys, both in climate and soil, will go far toward giving her tobacco a reputation in the markets of the world that could scarcely be attained elsewhere in this country.

"Florida tobacco should make a reputation for itself, for there is a certain flavor and aroma possessed by it that is both desirable and agreeable, and we think it will find much favor with the smoker when properly introduced, as the experiments thus far made in the raising of tobacco leave no doubt in our minds that the industry can be made a success, and also assume vast proportions.

"The culture of tobacco in Florida is not new; it is but the revival of what almost seems a lost industry. But never was there a more favorable time than the present for its renewal on a large scale."

FLORIDA FRUITS.

Too much cannot be said of Florida's delicious fruits. The orange is considered the most profitable, as well as the most prolific, of our fruits. The praise of the Florida orange has been sung in every land and clime, and the new varieties which have been brought forward in the last few years make it possible to enjoy this delightful product of our sunny clime from the first of November until the first of August.

VARIETIES OF THE ORANGE.

In growing the orange it is as well to plant varieties which have been tested and known to be prolific and desirable as to plant seedlings, which possibly may not prove satisfactory when

Take the SAVANNAH, FLORIDA & WESTERN RAILWAY,
The Through Car and Short Line to and from Florida.

LITTLE BRO'S
Fertilizer and Phosphate Co.

Jacksonville, Fla.

———LATE———

South Florida Fertilizer Co.,
ORLANDO, FLA.

OWING to the success met with in Orlando, we have moved to Jacksonville, where we have decided to commence in business on a larger scale, and are prepared to supply our customers with our various well-known brands for Orange Trees, Pineapples, Peach Trees, Grapes and Vegetables. We keep in stock a large quantity of material, such as Sulphate of Potash, Kainit, Salt, Cotton Seed Meal, Cotton Seed Hull Ash, Hardwood Ashes, etc., etc., which we are prepared to sell at the lowest market prices.

We will mix any desired formula at the shortest notice.

We shall be pleased to submit our Catalogues, showing prices and description of our goods.

All correspondence promptly attended to.

LITTLE BRO'S FERTILIZER & PHOSPHATE CO..

Box 749, Jacksonville, Fla.

Office 24 E. Bay St.
Factory, South Jacksonville.

☞ Visit Green Cove Springs, a delightful Retreat for the Tourist, Invalid, Immigrant or Sportsman. Excellent Hotels, the Borden Parks, Fine Fishing and Hunting. Reached by Steamer or Train.

they come into bearing. For the past eight or ten years much attention has been given by amateurs and professional fruit growers to selecting the varieties which promise the best, and the result has been that we are now enabled to select varieties which give a wide range in the time of ripening, and almost every quality desirable. We propose to give a short description of a few well known varieties, which we believe will meet the requirements of all orange growers, and be satisfactory to all concerned. We shall begin with the one we believe to be the best, embracing all the desirable qualities, and continue the list, pointing out the different features as they vary in comparison.

MAGNUM BONUM.—Large to very large; skin moderately thin, tough, smooth and glossy; pulp fine, tender, melting, juicy, sweet and vinous. The membranes inclosing the juice cells are remarkably thin, and leave but little residue on eating the orange. Ripens in January, and is prime first of February. *The best.*

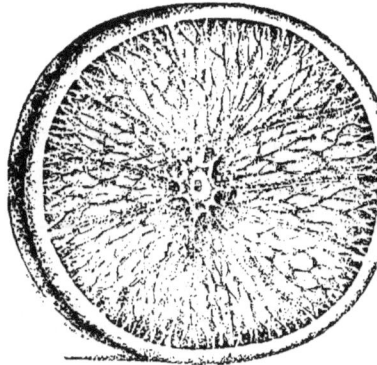
SECTION OF THE HOMOSASSA.

HOMOSASSA.—Medium size; skin very thin, smooth, tough and glossy; pulp very fine, remarkably juicy, sweet and delicious. Ripens in December, and is prime in January; early and prolific bearer.

HIGGINS.—Similar to Homosassa, but ripens later.

NONPAREIL.—Above medium; bright color; skin moderately thin; pulp tender and melting; juice sub-acid and vinous. Ripens last of January and February; an early bearer.

OLD VINI.—Above medium in size, oval in shape; skin rather thick and rough; pulp somewhat coarse; juice sweet and remarkable for a sprightly, aromatic flavor. This is the standard for flavor, and bears the same relation to the orange that the Seckle pear does to all other pears. Ripens in January, and is prime in February.

NAVEL.—Size very large; skin rough, thick and tough; conical in shape; blossom end presents the appearance of the human navel, hence its name; and this appearance is nothing more nor less than a small orange inclosed and nearly surrounded

Take the SAVANNAH, FLORIDA & WESTERN RAILWAY,
The Through Car and Short Line to and from Florida.

ANDERSON & TOWNSEND,

142 EAST BAY ST.,

MANUFACTURERS OF

Cypress :·: Shingles.

PINE AND OAK WOOD

Cut to Order and Delivered to any Part of the City.

TELEPHONE 152.

W. S. BUNTING,

— DEALER IN —

Fish, Oysters, Green Turtle,

Cedar Key and Rocky Point Oysters.

HARTRIDGE'S WHARF,

TELEPHONE 264.   JACKSONVILLE, FLA.

☞ Visit Green Cove Springs, a delightful Retreat for the Tourist, Invalid, Immigrant, or Sportsman. Excellent Hotels, the Borden Parks, Fine Fishing and Hunting. Reached by Steamer or Train.

by the pulp of the mother orange. Pulp very fine, melting, tender, juicy, sweet, and good flavor. Ripens in February, and is valuable on account of its late ripening, keeping and carrying qualities. A very early bearer. Many believe it to be a shy bearer, but as the tree grows to maturity we believe it will prove to be among the best. This variety will always be popular, in consequence of its superior qualities when mature, and from the fact that none other can be substituted for it. It carries its own unchangeable "trade mark." Tree a fair grower, nearly thornless, and fruit nearly seedless.

TARDIFF.—Size large, or above medium; skin rather rough and moderately thick and tough; pulp fine, tender, melting; juice sweet and good flavor. Ripens in March and April, and prime in May and June. A good ordinary orange, but valuable on account of late ripening and carrying qualities.

DUMMITT.—Large, bright, handsome shape; skin very thin and tender; pulp fine, melting, juicy, very sweet and vinous. One of the best, but, in consequence of its thin, tender skin, it requires great care in handling to prevent bruising. A poor shipper. Ripens in January, and, when in its prime, one of the most delicious oranges known.

MEDITERRANEAN SWEET.—This variety is of medium or large size; oval in shape; medium thin skin; pulp a little coarse, juicy and very sweet. Ripens in February. Tree a fair grower, but branches are inclined to droop and become dwarfish. Branches entirely thornless, and fruit nearly seedless; an early and prolific bearer; will bear the second year after budding on five-year-old stock. Valuable for its early prolific bearing, thornless branches, late ripening and carrying qualities.

BEACH'S No. 1 EGG.—Medium size; thin skin; pulp rather coarse, juicy, sweet and delicious. Ripens first of November, and prime in December. Valuable for its early ripening, sweetness, and keeping and carrying qualities. Probably the best early ripening good orange.

PHILLIPS' BITTER SWEET.—Medium to large size; thin skin; pulp tender, juicy, slightly sub-acid, bitter and aromatic. Ripens from April to June. A good summer fruit. Tree is, doubtless, a hybrid of the sweet and wild orange, and the branches are free from thorns.

MANDARIN—TANGERINE—KID GLOVE.—Oranges classed under this heading, undoubtedly, belong to a distinct

Take the SAVANNAH, FLORIDA & WESTERN RAILWAY,
The Through Car and Short Line to and from Florida.

THE BERGNER & ENGEL

BREWING COMPANY,

OF

PHILADELPHIA, PA.

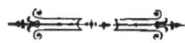

FLORIDA DEPOT.

Jacksonville, Fla.

P. SATTELKAU,
Manager.

Tannhæuser Beer,

(FANCY BREWING).

Brewing Unexcelled. Has taken the Highest Prizes Wherever exhibited. Last Award was taken at

PARIS EXPOSITION, 1889.

☞ Visit Green Cove Springs, a delightful Retreat for the Tourist, Invalid, Immigrant or Sportsman. Excellent Hotels, the Borden Parks, Fine Fishing and Hunting. Reached by Steamer and Train.

species of the citrus family, as they have very few, if any, characteristics of the common oranges. Small to medium size, flattened at the blossom end, or shaped like a tomato; skin rather smooth, ribbed, and, when the fruit is mature, it parts readily from the pulp. Pulp rather coarse, sections separate readily without breaking the membrane; juicy, sweet, aromatic and delicious. Ripens in December, and prime in January. There are numberous varieties of this fine fruit, from the very small to large; skin usually bright or orange, with small dark speckles, and the odor, on breaking the skin, is strong, pungent and disagreeable. Dancy's Tangerine differs from the ordinary fruit only in color of the rind, which is a deep crimson. Tree usually very thorny, leaves small, willow-shaped, and branches slender and dark hue.

SATSUMA.—This is a late importation from Japan. Fruit much larger than the foregoing, but of same species and many of the characteristics. Tree a slow grower, branches drooping, thornless, and fruit seedless; early and prolific bearer; bears second year after budding on four or five-year-old stock. Tree very hardy, leaves large and leathery, and will stand a low degree of temperature without injury. On account of its hardiness, disposition to dwarf, fine quality of fruit, early ripening— December—this should become a popular variety, and be largely planted.

There are many other varieties of the orange which are, doubtless, equal, in many respects, to some we have mentioned above, but these we know to be all that is claimed for them, and a person owning a grove planted with a due proportion of the varieties here described need look no farther for quality of fruit. Here we have varieties ripening from October to April, which ought to satisfy the taste and mind of all lovers and growers of the golden fruit.

PEACHES.

The introduction of the Chinese strain of peaches and their offspring in the last few years, together with their marked success wherever planted in the State, has given great impetus to tree planting, and hundreds of acres have been set out, which have generally come into bearing the second year.

The small Peen-to peach of several years ago has been brought up, by cultivation, to nearly twice its former size, and of a delicious flavor, having none of the bitter taste which formerly characterized this fruit. This variety is the first to ripen,

Take the SAVANNAH, FLORIDA & WESTERN RAILWAY,
The Through Car and Short Line to and from Florida.

A. B. VANCE,
Book and Job Printing
IN ALL ITS BRANCHES.
HOTEL WORK A SPECIALTY.
MANUFACTURER OF RUBBER STAMPS AND STENCILS.
Paper Bags, Butter Dishes, Grocery, Butcher and Butter Paper,
DAY AND PASS BOOKS, ETC.
NEW YORK PRICES ON THE ABOVE.
72½ W. Bay St.,   Jacksonville, Fla.

FRESH STOCK.   **LARGE VARIETY.**

M. FOSTER & SONS,
CAMPBELL'S ADDITION, JACKSONVILLE,
MANUFACTURERS OF
PURE CONFECTIONERY,
WHOLESALE AND RETAIL.
All Goods Guaranteed.
PURE GOODS.   **LOWEST PRICES.**

ROBBINS & HARWICK,
ATTORNEYS-AT-LAW,
NOTARY PUBLIC.
64½ WEST BAY STREET,
Jacksonville, Florida.

N. BACKENSTOE,
Cor. State and Newnan Streets,

Fancy and Family Groceries,
Tobacco & Cigars, Hay and Grain.
LOWEST PRICES FOR FIRST-CLASS GOODS.

☞ Visit Green Cove Springs, a delightful Retreat for the Tourist, Invalid Immigrant or Sportsman. Excellent Hotels, the Borden Parks, Fine Fishing and Hunting. Reached by Steamer or Train.

commencing the last of April or first of May, and is closely followed by the Honey.

Only those who have tasted this favorite peach, picked ripe from the tree, can have any idea of its quality. As its name implies, it is sweet, and when fully ripe fairly melts in the mouth. Apricots and nectarines have been tried with success, especially in the north of Florida, and the trees are finding their way into nearly every orchard.

THE ANGEL PEACH SEEDLING OF THE PEEN-TO.

No fruit has been introduced into our State that has been such a happy surprise as the Kelsey plum. This fruit has been grown in California for several years, and there pronounced the King of Plums, and the result in this State, so far, bears out that reputation.

The tree commences to bear two years from planting when properly cared for, and the yield is simply enormous. Trees at this age have borne such enormous crops that the limbs had to be supported to keep them from breaking and sweeping the ground.

Take the **SAVANNAH, FLORIDA & WESTERN RAILWAY,**
The Through Car and Short Line to and from Florida.

Raymond D. Knight & Co.,

(Successors to Mumby, Stockton & Knight),

IMPORTERS, WHOLESALE AND RETAIL DEALERS IN

Crockery, China, Glass and Earthenware.

Stoves, Tinware and Housefurnishing Goods.

Sterling Silver Plated Ware and Rich Cut Glass.

SOLE STATE AGENTS FOR THE

Celebrated Monitor Oil Stoves,
Globe Incandescent Lamps,
Iceberg Chief Refrigerators,
White Mountain Ice Cream Freezers.

13 West Bay, and 14 and 16 West Forsyth Sts.,
JACKSONVILLE, FLA.

☞ Visit Green Cove Springs, a delightful Retreat for the Tourist, Invalid, Immigrant or Sportsman. Excellent Hotels, the Borden Parks, Fine Fishing and Hunting. Reached by Steamer or Train.

Other new varieties of plums are being introduced, with every prospect of success. The Chickasaw strain does well here, and furnishes a variety not only in fruit, but in time of ripening.

The Loquat (*Japan Medlar*) differs from the other varieties of plums in being an evergreen tree, and producing its fruit in January, if the winter is mild, and later if severe. The tree is grown farther north for its beautiful foliage, while here we have

KELSEY JAPAN PLUM

both the foliage and fruit. The fruit is about the size of the Wild Goose plum; oblong, of a light yellow color; acid, and excellent quality.

THE JAPAN PERSIMMON

is grown in a number of varieties. They are of a most excellent quality, and command the highest prices in the market. The trees do well, and generally come into bearing the second year.

Take the SAVANNAH, FLORIDA & WESTERN RAILWAY,
The Through Car and Short Line to and from Florida.

EMERY & CO.,

11 EAST AND 47 WEST BAY STREET,

Jacksonville, Florida.

We are daily receiving large quantities of Boots and Shoes for winter wear. Correct styles and at lowest prices. We have knocked competition out of time, and are offering the best stock of

BOOTS, SHOES AND SLIPPERS,

FOR PERSONS OF ALL AGES AND SIZES.

OUR GOODS ARE

BEST For the Rich, because we offer a choice of the finest manufactures in the country.

BEST For the Poor, because we can show a good quality at prices to suit your pocket.

BEST For the Young and Old, Healthy and Weak, because we give an easy fit at an easy price.

OUR PRICES WILL FIT YOUR POCKET.
OUR GOODS WILL FIT YOUR FEET.

Everybody can rely upon a cordial reception and satisfactory bargains at our stores.

EMERY & CO.,

11 EAST AND 47 WEST BAY STREET.

☞ Visit Green Cove Springs, a delightful Retreat for the Tourist, Invalid Immigrant or Sportsman. Excellent Hotels, the Borden Parks, Fine Fishing and Hunting. Reached by Steamer or Train.

THE PINEAPPLE.

The profitable cultivation of the pineapple must be practically confined to that portion of the State generally exempt from even slight frosts. With some protection they are raised as far north as Orange County, and in some favored positions have been long grown even where slight frosts are common; but we may be sure the pine will always continue to assert its tropical character.

The English gardeners of the last century thought it the height of horticultural skill to produce pines in their cool, damp climate under glass, and, as usual, the directions they have left us are so conflicting as to be far from edifying. And we meet with a similar conflict of ideas here in regard to the culture of

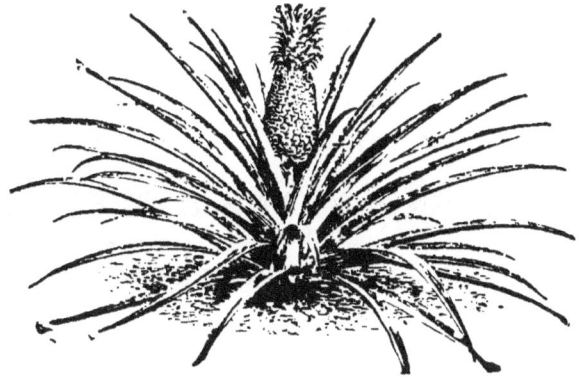

PINEAPPLE PLANT AND FRUIT.

the pine. It is not easy, without more experience than we have, to sift out the wheat from the chaff. There are a few things that seem very well settled, and these shall have our notice.

It is evident here that the high, light, dry, sandy soil is preferable to the shell, or even the richest hammock lands, for the culture of the pine. Also, that the shelter belts, so much needed by the banana, are positively injurious to the pine. This is specially true when the shelter belts are on the east or north sides of a pine field. They are not injured by the shade, but by the hot sun and still air.

While there are many varieties of the pine clamoring for notice, there seems as yet to be no one that can be trusted to take the place of the common Red Spanish for a general crop. There are larger, sweeter and more delicious pines in experimental cultivation, and yet, as far as we know, we have to name each with

Take the **SAVANNAH, FLORIDA & WESTERN RAILWAY,**
The Through Car and Short Line to and from Florida.

ASHLEY & CROSBY,
DEALERS IN
FINE FAMILY GROCERIES,
CANDIES, NUTS,
Cigars, Tobacco and Country Produce.
Also, FINE STOCK OF FRESH MEATS.
EVERYTHING AT REASONABLE PRICES.
Corner Brough and Maggie Streets.   FREE DELIVERY.

S. J. BOUKNIGHT,
LAND AND LOAN BROKER,
AND
GENERAL DEALER IN CITY PROPERTY.
5½ EAST BAY STREET.
JACKSONVILLE, FLA.

NEGOTIATING LOANS A SPECIALTY.

THE OLD RELIABLE
SQUARE DEALING CLOTHING HOUSE!

AARON ZACHARIAS,
WHOLESALE AND RETAIL DEALER IN
MEN'S AND BOYS' CLOTHING,
Hats, Caps, Gent's Furnishing Goods,
Trunks, Valises, Umbrellas.

---

17 W. Bay St.,   13 Lemon St.,   Magnolia St.,
Jacksonville, Fla.   Palatka, Fla.   Ocala, Fla.

☞ Visit Green Cove Springs, a delightful Retreat for the Tourist, Invalid, Immigrant or Sportsman. Excellent Hotels, the Borden Parks, Fine Fishing and Hunting. Reached by Steamer and Train.

a qualifying but. It may give us a hint, perhaps, to simply say that while the old pine growers upon the keys are always ready to sell us new varieties at speculative prices, they plant their own acres with Red Spanish. Very likely this is not an accident or a short-sighted economy. From their stand-point they only choose what to them seems the better.

Our experience encourages the planting of slips and suckers immediately after picking, not leaving them to dry, as is sometimes done, for weeks. And in so doing we prefer not to trim them. This is opposed to the general practice. Again, suckers are sold at higher prices than the slips, but for our planting the latter are preferable.

New plantations are made usually from August to October. The slips, growing out at the base of the fruit; the suckers, which spring from the axils of the leaves near the ground, and the crowns, from the apex of the fruit, are all used in making new plantations. When the fruit is gathered the slips are left for a month, or more, upon the stem to grow. Such slips as are unavoidably broken off with the fruit, if slips are scarce, can be planted immediately, though they may be small. Each plant will send up from one to three suckers from near the ground. The one nearest the ground should be left for the next crop, the others removed and planted. A part of the suckers will produce small fruit the following season, and, as a result, such plants are weak. The slips will require eighteen months to develop fruit, but the plants will be strong, and the fruit large. The first crop is usually the most even and abundant. How long a plantation can be kept in profitable bearing is not yet certain. On the common white sand, with only ordinary care, three good successive crops have been grown, with present prospects of a fair fourth crop.

The culture of the pine is extending very rapidly along the eastern coast of Florida from Eden, on the Indian River, south. Many acres are already planted on Lake Worth. For several years the growing of pines has been the leading industry upon the keys. Unfortunately, most of the earlier plantations of pines upon this coast were made upon unsuitable soil. Our people are beginning to realize the importance of a more intensive system of culture. This promises well for our future.

GUAVAS.

The guava is grown to quite an extent, especially in the southern part of the State, where the crop is truly wonderful. The guava is one of the finest fruits grown for jelly.

Take the SAVANNAH, FLORIDA & WESTERN RAILWAY,
The Through Car and Short Line to and from Florida.

SHORT ACCOUNTS MAKE LONG FRIENDS.

J. W. WHITE,

The largest Advertising man in the State. All kinds of Advertising done promptly. Correspondent for newspapers in different sections of the country.

JACKSONVILLE, FLA.

WHAT CAN I DO FOR YOY?   *JUDICIOUS ADVERTISING PAYS.*

THE CARLETON HOUSE
Barber Shop and Bathing Establishment.
HOT, COLD AND SHOWER BATHS.
ONE OF THE
FINEST TONSORIAL PARLORS
IN THE SOUTH, AND ONE PRICE ONLY.
No. 35 East Bay St., Jacksonville, Fla.
C. L. DECKER, Proprietor.

BUY OF
The Leading Furniture House of the State,
AND SAVE MONEY.
Largest Stock South of Baltimore.

Latest Designs in Parlor and Bedroom Suites in Antique Oak, Mahogany, Cherry, Walnut and Imitation. Hall Stands, Bed Lounges, Willow, Reed and Rattan Goods, Desks of all kinds and Styles.

We sell you the Best Goods for the Least Money.
HOUSEFURNISHING GOODS OF ALL KINDS.

Carpets, Mattings, Curtains, Window Shades, Hanging Lamps, China and Crockery Sets, Tin Toilet Sets, Mirrors, Curtain Poles and Brackets. Hotels, Boarding Houses, Ships, Steamers, Offices and Private Residences Furnished from Top to Bottom.

40 and 42 W. Bay St., Jacksonville, Fla.
Correspondence Solicited.

☞ Visit Green Cove Springs, a delightful Retreat for the Tourist, Invalid, Immigrant or Sportsman. Excellent Hotels, the Borden Parks, Fine Fishing and Hunting. Reached by Steamer or Train.

THE NORTON

Take the SAVANNAH, FLORIDA & WESTERN RAILWAY,
The Through Car and Short Line to and from Florida.

SEASON OF 1890-91.

THE ACME OPEN ALL THE YEAR THE ACME

ACCOMMODATIONS FOR 100 GUESTS.

Furnished Rooms 50c. to $1.00 per Day, $2.00 to $5.00 per Week.

Restaurant in connection on European and American Plan.

Refitted and Refurnished with entirely new Furniture throughout.

Centrally located, convenient to Depot and Boat Landings.

No. 111 WEST BAY STREET, JACKSONVILLE, FLA.

H. A. BURT, Proprietor.

☞ Visit Green Cove Springs, a delightful Retreat for the Tourist, Invalid, Immigrant or Sportsman. Excellent Hotels, the Borden Parks, Fine Fishing and Hunting. Reached by Steamer or Train.

PEARS.

Very large orchards of LeConte pears are being set out, especially in that section of the State known as Middle Florida. Other varieties are being tested, but are not as prolific as the LeConte.

FIGS.

This is rightly considered as one of Florida's neglected fruits, for it is known to the oldest inhabitant in some way or other. New varieties have been introduced, and it is claimed that we have the true fig of commerce. The White Adriatic is a most delicious fruit, and is good for either drying or table use. The drying and preserving of figs should be one of Florida's industries. As the fruit becomes better known, and the little care required to raise it realized, the evaporation of figs must become a business that will retain many a dollar that is now sent to foreign lands.

GRAPES.

After patient experimenting, a number of varieties of grapes have been found to do exceedingly well, and all over the State growers are increasing their vineyards, and, although a new industry, bids fair to be a source of great revenue to the State, as they ripen early in our climate, and always demand a good price.

BANANAS.

The banana is another of our beautiful fruit-bearing plants, and the numerous varieties may be found in nearly every garden from Jacksonville to the southernmost part of the State. The two principal varieties grown are the Horse and the Lady Finger. The plant often grows to a great height, presenting a most beautiful appearance.

MANGO.

There are several varieties of this fruit, as with others, but the tree, did it bear no fruit, would be very desirable for its beautiful shape and rich foliage, the leaves forming a star at the end of every twig. The fruit has a large seed, and the pulp is filled with a coarse fiber. The kinds having little fiber are considered the best. This variety is known in the West Indies as No. 11. There are quite a number of varieties grown in the southern part of Florida, but the one which seems to be the favorite is the Apricot mango.

Take the SAVANNAH, FLORIDA & WESTERN RAILWAY,
The Through Car and Short Line to and from Florida.

Established New York, 1854.   Established Jacksonville, Fla., 1873.

THOMAS NOONEY & SONS,

WHOLESALE COMMISSION MERCHANTS

IN, AND SHIPPERS OF,

Foreign and Domestic Fruits and Produce,

12 EAST BAY STREET,

181 Reade Street, New York.   JACKSONVILLE, FLA.

All orders for Shipping promptly attended to. Consignments of Produce and Fruits are solicited.

RETURNS MADE ON DAY OF SALE.

Thos. Nooney.   Chas A. Nooney.   Frank Nooney.

NEW INDEPENDENT LINE STEAMERS.

MANATEE.   MARY DRAPER.

Jacksonville, Hibernia, Orange Park, Mandarin, Magnolia, Switzerland, and all way landings.

LEAVE JACKSONVILLE at - - 2.30 p. m. Daily.
LEAVE GREEN COVE at - - 6.30 a. m. Daily.

Steamer Mary Draper for charter for Hunting, Fishing and Excursion Parties.

Office and Pier, foot of Main Street, Jacksonville.
C. E. GARNER, General Manager.

☞ Visit Green Cove Springs, a delightful Retreat for the Tourist, Invalid, Immigrant, or Sportsman. Excellent Hotels, the Borden Parks, Fine Fishing and Hunting. Reached by Steamer or Train.

BANANA GROVE

Take the SAVANNAH, FLORIDA & WESTERN RAILWAY,
The Through Car and Short Line to and from Florida.

WILLIAM CLARKE

52 W. FORSYTH ST.,

Plumber and Gas Fitter.

Fine Gas Fixtures and Plumbing Materials of all kinds.

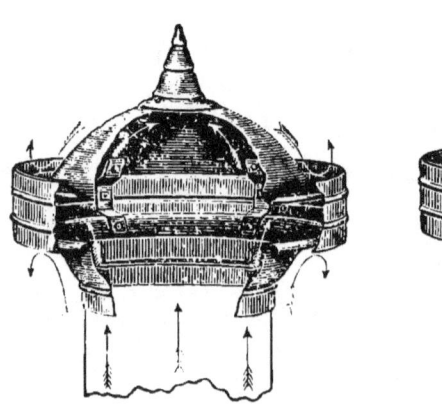 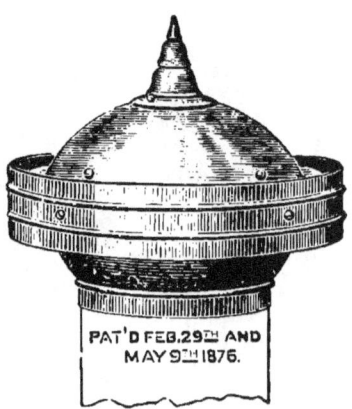

PAT'D FEB.29TH AND MAY 9TH 1876.

Agent for the Globe Ventilator and Chimney Cap

For ventilation of public and private buildings, school houses, churches, mills, machine shops, round houses, railroad cars, etc.

Downward drafts of chimneys and car lamps cured. Noiseless, simple, durable, stationary, storm proof, handsome and cheap. Also, agent for

TUERK WATER MOTOR,

For running light machinery of all kinds. The best in the market.

☞ Visit Green Cove Springs, a delightful Retreat for the Tourist, Invalid, Immigrant or Sportsman. Excellent Hotels, the Borden Parks, Fine Fishing and Hunting. Reached by Rail or Steamer.

PAWPAW.

(Curica papaya.)

This is not the fruit known by that name in the Southern and Eastern States. It is a native of South America, and is sometimes called the Bread Fruit tree. This fruit is not grown so much for its eating qualities as for its wonderful properties. However, it is sometimes eaten raw, and has a flavor something like the muskmelon. The milky juice is used in cooking all kinds of tough meats. A little of the juice is put in with the meat and stewed for a few minutes, making it very tender and palatable. Meat laid between its bruised leaves is said to absorb enough of its juice to make it tender, especially with steaks. Its medicinal qualities are equally wonderful, the juice of a green fruit being one of the best vermifuges known, and the leaves are used in the West Indies in washing, instead of soap.

ANONA.

There are some forty varieties of this family, and Florida lays claim to some of the best, such as the sugar apple (*A. squamosa*), sour sap (*A. muricata*), cherimoya or Japan apple (*A. cherimolia*), and others. The sugar apple could be grown over a considerable portion of the State, as it seldom grows over four feet high, and could be protected from cold the same as the guava.

Arrowroot and cassava are two of the best starch-yielding plants in the United States, and they grow to perfection here.

The date palm is one of the most magnificent fruit-bearing trees within our borders. Its long, graceful, verdant, ever-changing branches make it a beauty to behold. It is grown as far north as St. Augustine, and gives a rich and picturesque appearance to every garden in which it is planted. There is no fruit tree on the continent that combines such rare beauty and rich foliage with its fruit-producing qualities.

SAPODILLA.

(Achras Sapota.)

This fruit is grown somewhat extensively along the coast of South Florida and upon the keys. Its profitable culture will, doubtless, be confined to about the same limits with the cocoanut. The tree grows at first quite slowly, but when once established it grows more rapidly, and soon makes a conical tree about twenty feet in height. The leaves are thick, smooth, and very

Take the SAVANNAH, FLORIDA & WESTERN RAILWAY,
The Through Car and Short Line to and from Florida.

C. A. GAMBRILL MANUFACTURING CO.,
PROPRIETORS OF THE
Patapsco * Flouring * Mills,
BALTIMORE, MD.
ESTABLISHED 1774.

MANUFACTURERS OF

Patapsco's Superlative Patent,
THE PREMIER FLOUR OF AMERICA,

AND

Medora Highest Grade of Winter Wheat.

Bread made from these Flours cannot be excelled for richness and sweetness by any other Flour in the United States. Try them. Ask your Grocer for them, and take no other.

JAS. H. BURST, State Agent,

P. O. Box 158. JACKSONVILLE, FLA.

D. T. GEROW. FRANK CLARKSON.

Gerow & Clarkson,
WHOLESALE AND RETAIL DEALERS IN

ILLUMINATING AND LUBRICATING
OILS AND GREASES.
RAILROAD AND MILL SUPPLIES.
PURE LINSEED OIL AND TURPENTINE.

Railroad Oils and Greases a Specialty.

Jacksonville, Fla.

Send for Price List.

☞ Visit Green Cove Springs, a delightful Retreat for the Tourist, Invalid, Immigrant or Sportsman. Excellent Hotels, the Borden Parks, Fine Fishing and Hunting. Reached by Steamer or Train.

glossy, with a marked tendency to form dense terminal clusters. The flowers are small. The fruit is formed on terminal shoots, frequently in clusters of four and five. The fruit varies much in size, and often somewhat in quality. Externally it resembles an English russet apple, while the flesh is not unlike the most delicate of sweet pears, with a slight granulation surrounding a few glossy seeds—from one to five. This fruit, picked in a green state, is frequently sent from the Bahamas to Jacksonville, and, perhaps, to some other points on the Atlantic coast; but in that condition it is very unlike the sapodilla as gathered in a mature state from our own trees. Like the banana, the cocoanut and the guava, the sapodilla is a continuous bearer, though it is not equally productive throughout the year.

Hitherto this fruit has been propagated exclusively from the seed. Variation, then, is the rule, somewhat in quality and more in its size and form. The intrinsic value of this fruit certainly warrants the most careful attention to its improvement.

SUGAR APPLE.
(*Anona Squamosa.*)

Among the anonas are found some very delicate and valuable fruits. These trees, varying greatly in character, seem to be natives of all tropical regions; and it is not improbable that we may yet secure some valuable additions to the anona fruit list.

The sugar apple is, so far, the best known and most popular of all the anonas. It is quite extensively grown upon the keys and along the east and west coasts of Florida; in many places so far north as to be frequently killed back by frost. It is little more than a shrub, seldom growing higher than fifteen feet, and frequently producing fruit in abundance when only four or five feet high. It can be so pruned as to be easily protected from slight cold, and hence can be grown for home use much farther north than any other anona. The tree is dormant for a short time in the winter months, but with us is not quite deciduous. Though found everywhere in southernmost Florida, it has been grown, so far, only for home use, excepting upon the keys. The fruit is very delicate, and will require as careful and prompt handling as strawberries. It should be noted that a recent successful shipment of this fruit has been made by express from Lake Worth to Philadelphia. With the improvements that are sure soon to come, this fact gives us a better prospect for the future. The fruit resembles a shortened pine cone three or four

Take the SAVANNAH, FLORIDA & WESTERN RAILWAY,
The Through Car and Short Line to and from Florida.

A. M. KANTOF,
—THE—
Merchant Tailor,
AT —
30 Hogan St., between Bay and Forsyth.

Ranks foremost among the Tailors of this city, and his stock of Imported and Domestic Goods cannot be excelled in the city. He makes a specialty in fitting pants, and guarantees a fit every time.

MAYNARD,
TICKET :: BROKER,
Union Ticket Office, 95 West Bay Street,
Corner Bay and Hogan,
JACKSONVILLE, FLORIDA.
Lowest Rates to 50,000 points in the United States.
EXCURSION TICKETS BOUGHT AND SOLD.

MASON & CO.,
Wholesale and Retail Dealers in Foreign and Domestic
Wines, Liquors, Cigars, Etc.

Wholesale Dealers in Milwaukee, Bergner & Engel, and Cook Brewing Company's Beers.

Sole Agents for Wallace's and Land of Flowers Pure Rye Whiskeys.

OFFICE AND WAREHOUSE, 115 WEST BAY ST.

All orders must be accompanied by Postal Note, Money Order, Registered Letter, Bank Check, Money sent by Express, or satisfactory City Reference must be given.

We will pay the charges on all Money Packages addressed to us by express.

☞ Visit Green Cove Springs, a delightful Retreat for the Tourist, Invalid, Immigrant or Sportsman. Excellent Hotels, the Borden Parks, Fine Fishing and Hunting. Reached by Steamer or Train.

inches in diameter, with a yellowish green exterior, and has a very sweet cream-white pulp, which is best eaten with a spoon. Most people soon learn to relish it very much, and are inclined to give it a very high place as a dessert fruit.

TAMARIND.
(Tamarindus Indica.)

This tree is worthy of more attention than has hitherto been given it. It is strictly tropical, and should be planted only where there is little danger of frost. As an ornamental tree it is extensively planted in all tropical countries. Its delicate acacia-like leaves, closing at night, together with the density of its shade, bring it out in agreeable and striking contrast with other tropical plants and trees. There can scarcely be a more beautiful tree than the tamarind. From our past experience we may plant it anywhere in South Florida where the mango and sapodilla do not suffer from the frost. But this tree is of still greater interest, because it yields an abundance of valuable and agreeable fruit. This grows in large, thick pods containing a large quantity of delicate acid, used as the basis of an acid drink much esteemed in fevers. These pods grow in large clusters, and seemingly crowd the leaves from the branches. If carefully picked they can be kept for two or three months in their natural state, and there seems to be no reason why they cannot be supplied thus to Northern customers. And there certainly is no good reason why this most delicate, healthful and agreeable fruit acid should not be in more general demand.

Other fruits may be grown throughout the State, but the list here produced includes the more important, and will serve, we trust, to give the reader some idea of the fruits of fair Florida.

PHOSPHATES.

THE recent discovery of rich phosphate beds in Florida created an excitement equal to the discovery of gold on the Pacific coast, in 1849. The discovery means fabulous wealth, greater prosperity, an expanding commerce.

Considered in its relation to science, the discovery is not less important. It has upset all the accepted theories of the geological formation of Florida, and opened a broad field of investigation for the geologist, the paleontologist and the antiquary. Here

Take the SAVANNAH, FLORIDA & WESTERN RAILWAY,
The Through Car and Short Line to and from Florida.

HIDITCH STEAM LAUNDRY CO.
44 WEST FORSYTH STREET.

Every Description of Laundry Work done in the best possible manner.

Special Attention Given to Orders Required at Short Notice.

GOODS CALLED FOR AND DELIVERED.

TELEPHONE No. 157.

MERRYDAY & PAINE,
No. 41 EAST BAY STREET,
OPPOSITE POST-OFFICE.

PIANOS, ORGANS,
Guitars, Violins, Banjos,
Sheet Music, Strings, Etc.

THE CHELSEA
(Formerly Mrs. Henderson's),

Corner Monroe and Main Sts., Jacksonville, Fla.

R. NEDDO, Proprietor.

CENTRALLY LOCATED.
ALL MODERN CONVENIENCES.
ROOMS EN SUITE OR SINGLE.
HOT AND COLD BATHS ON EACH FLOOR.

This House will be conducted as a Fashionable Boarding House on the Hotel Plan.

RATES $2.00 PER DAY.

Table Board, $6.00 per Week.   Rooms, According to Location.

☞ Visit Green Cove Springs, a delightful Retreat for the Tourist, Invalid, Immigrant or Sportsman. Excellent Hotels, the Borden Parks, Fine Fishing and Hunting. Reached by Steamer or Train.

are many strange forms of animal life which played their little parts in the great drama of progressive creation, and made their final exits before man, "the heavy villain" of the play, made his appearance on the world's stage.

The great wealth which has so suddenly made its appearance is known in commerce as phosphate rock, bone phosphate, natural phosphate or simple phosphate, is bone phosphate of lime in combination with varying percentages of silica, magnesia, iron, alumina, etc.

The marine god Proteus could not assume more forms than does phosphate. Acquaintance with one, or a number of varieties, does not enable one to recognize other forms; chemical analysis is the only sure guide. When occurring in six-sided prisms, more or less transparent, it is called apatite. This name, however, is applied to other forms, as in Canada it is given to a soft, granular substance, greatly resembling pure sand, and known locally as "sugar phosphate." Referring to the phosphate fields on the Ottawa River, in Canada, a writer in the *Scientific American* says: "The phosphate itself varies much, according to locality. It is found in crystals sometimes of large dimensions; in masses, varying from compact to coarse granular; in strata of a lamillar texture, and in a friable form. The colors are very varied, consisting of green of different shades; blue, red, and brown of all shades; yellow, white and cream-colored. Occasionally beautiful crystals are met with, large and perfect at both ends. * * * * In one of the mines on the Lievre crystals of gigantic size have been met with, some weighing individually as much as one thousand pounds."

When occurring as the fossilized excrements of animals and birds, phosphate is known to geologists as coprolites (literally translated, petrified guano), and is called by miners "bird-lime." It consists usually of small white nodules, imbedded in a buff, more or less plastic, chalky matrix, the matrix itself being a lower grade of phosphate. Much of the Florida phosphate is of this kind, and it is not unusual to find samples in which the nodules show 75 to 80 per cent. and the matrix 65 to 70 per cent. of phosphate of lime. Within a mile of the depot at Bartow is a bed which gave 63 per cent. as the analysis of the *mass*, while the nodules alone assayed 84 per cent.

Occasionally deposits are found in which the nodules, if they exist at all, are not distinguishable from the matrix, the whole appearing as a compact, homogeneous mass, running through all the gradations of shade and color from buff or tan-

Take the SAVANNAH, FLORIDA & WESTERN RAILWAY.
The Through Car and Short Line to and from Florida.

THE CARLETON

MAHON, TOWNSHEND & AHERN, Proprietors.

BAY STREET, CORNER MARKET (OPP. P. O.) JACKSONVILLE, FLA.

CENTRALLY LOCATED.   ALL MODERN CONVENIENCES.

Table Supplied with the Best the Markets Afford.
TERMS, $3.00 PER DAY.
SPECIAL RATES BY THE WEEK.

Patronize Home Industry.

E. A. LINDSLEY,

BOX 526.   JACKSONVILLE, FLA.

Cigar Manufacturer,
LA ROSE FACTORY NO. 59.

This Factory is the only one in Duval County manufacturing Cigars from Tobacco grown here. GOODS GIVE PERFECT SATISFACTION.

☞ Visit Green Cove Springs, a delightful Retreat for the Tourist, Invalid, Immigrant or Sportsman. Excellent Hotels, the Borden Parks, Fine Fishing and Hunting. Reached by Steamer and Train.

color to pure white. It varies as much in consistence as in color, being soft, unctuous and plastic, or hard and tenacious, depending, apparently, upon the action of water or the degree of atmospheric exposure to which it has been subjected, or, probably, due to both influences.

The true nodular phosphate is found in egg-shaped or kidney-shaped nodules from an inch or less in diameter to a ton weight; of a grayish-white or bluish-black color, according to locality; usually rough, irregular and honey-combed externally, and sometimes presenting a somewhat vitrious appearance, not unlike slag from a zinc furnace.

Most of the phosphate rock of South Carolina is of that character, and it is found here in many places on the surface. Though samples quite rich in phosphoric acid have been found, I am not aware that any of this sort of rock has yet been shipped. It is used, to some extent, however, in macadamizing roads and streets.

Still another distinct form of phosphate is the pebble, or bone-pebble, as it is often termed; bluish-gray, dark blue and blue-black; amorphous nodules, of varying size, from a pea to a walnut. These pebbles, intermixed with sand, form immense beds and bars in Peace River, and scattered among them are the teeth, tusks, bones and scales of animals that roamed the earth and sported in the ocean depths when Florida (according to the generally accepted theory) was but a coral reef, struggling to lift its jagged head above the surf.

This is true bone phosphate, the pebbles being simply fragments of animal and fish bone, rounded and polished by attrition with the ever-shifting sands of the river for thousands of years. It is of a very high grade, rarely containing more than one per cent. of alumina, and remarkably free from other contaminating substances.

In this particular variety of plant food we have an eternal and everlasting monopoly, for the only extensive deposit of pebble phosphate in the known world is in Florida, and here the supply is simply inexhaustible.

It will bring millions of dollars into the State, with prospectors from all parts of the world. Valuable finds are reported daily; manufactories with the latest and most improved labor-saving devises are being erected in all phosphate sections. Lands which, a few months since, were regarded as worthless have since been sold as high as $350 per acre. The shipment of Florida phosphates to Europe is no longer an experiment, but a finan-

---

Take the SAVANNAH, FLORIDA & WESTERN RAILWAY,
The Through Car and Short Line to and from Florida.

DANIEL M. McINNIS,
FASHIONABLE MERCHANT TAILOR
24 OCEAN STREET,
Jacksonville, Fla.

All the Latest Styles in Foreign and Domestic Goods constantly on hand. Finest work and Lowest Prices in the City. Work guaranteed. Thirty-five years' experience. Twenty-two years in business in this City.

Cleaning, Dyeing and Repairing
PROMPTLY DONE.

TIVOLI BILLIARD AND POOL PARLOR,
66 West Bay St., Jacksonville, Fla.

THE LARGEST AND FINEST BILLIARD PARLOR IN THE SOUTH.
12 FIRST-CLASS TABLES.
Fine Line of Cigars and Tobacco.

THE EAGLE HAT
— AND —
Gents' Furnishing Goods House
Carries the Largest Stock of Hats in the State.
AGENT FOR KNOX & YOUMANS' HATS.
SIG. HESS,
15 West Bay St., Jacksonville, Fla.

☞ Visit Green Cove Springs, a delightful Retreat for the Tourist, Invalid, Immigrant or Sportsman. Excellent Hotels, the Borden Parks, Fine Fishing and Hunting. Reached by Steamer or Train.

cial success. The phosphates are all of a high grade, running from 65 to 90 per cent.

The Dunnellon Phosphate Company now employs over one thousand men on their works and mines. The shipments will, in a short time, average one hundred car loads per day.

The Marion County Phosphate Company are now employing hundreds of laborers, and expect to ship from sixty to one hundred car loads per day. Several other companies are pushing their works, and in a few weeks will be mining and shipping their ores.

The City of Jacksonville.

JACKSONVILLE has become famous all over the civilized world as the great winter resort of the sunny South. Built upon the splendid curve of the magnificent St. Johns River, whose bosom is the broadest, and whose sweep is the most majestic on the continent, Floridians may justly refer to it with pride and admiration as one of the chief ornaments of the State. The regularity and beauty of its streets; its beautiful gardens and unequalled shade trees—water and live oaks, magnolia, orange and pride of India; its mammoth hotels, popular Sub-Tropical and charming residences, and the number and rare attractions which surround it on every hand, justify its claim to preeminent beauty.

The city, in its human greed, has stolen much from the big-hearted and unsuspecting river. Acres of piling and rubbish have changed acres of water to land, on which imposing edifices stand, and over which the iron monster carries the tourist who seeks the great Florida metropolis for health, wealth or recreation. Long wharves run far out into the stream along the city's length, and it is to this that is due the well-known fact that the St. Johns, broad as it is at Jacksonville, is narrower here than at at any point between Palatka and the sea. But, for all this, the tourist who stands in swelling contemplation on its banks may well and justly feel that he looks upon the noblest river of his native land.

The natural beauty of the streets will draw forth the comely adjectives of the stranger. In sooth we are compelled to say that art has not aided nature as she should have done in these fair highways, and there is much work for art to do. But na-

Take the SAVANNAH, FLORIDA & WESTERN RAILWAY,
The Through Car and Short Line to and from Florida.

SEASON 1890-91.

WINDSOR HOTEL,

JACKSONVILLE, FLA.

Open December to May.

BOARD $4.00 PER DAY.

One Hundred Pleasant Rooms at $21.00 per Week, each Person.

Dogs Not Taken.   F. H. ORVIS.

PUTNAM HOUSE,

PALATKA, FLA.

BOARD $4.00 PER DAY.

One Hundred Pleasant Rooms at $21.00 per Week, each Person.

An abundant supply of soft water.

                                           E. C. & W. F. ORVIS, MANAGERS.

THE EQUINOX HOUSE,

MANCHESTER, VERMONT.

A delightful summer resort amongst the Green Mountains, 200 miles north of New York, 200 miles northwest of Boston, 50 miles north of Troy, 30 miles south of Rutland and 50 miles northeast of Saratoga, on the Pennington and Rutland Railway, midway between New York and Montreal.

Through Drawing Room and Sleeping Cars from New York via Hudson River Railroad.

                                                        F. H. ORVIS.

☞ Visit Green Cove Springs, a delightful Retreat for the Tourist, Invalid, Immigrant or Sportsman. Excellent Hotels, the Borden Parks, Fine Fishing and Hunting. Reached by Steamer or Train.

ture has been lavish in her hangings, decorations and fresco work. Think of street after street lined with stately, spreading live oaks that bend and meet over-head, making almost an arched and vaulted pathway of living green in well nigh perpetual shade. From these trees hang in rare profusion the sweeping and swaying tufts of moss, that always delight the Northern stranger's eye, and through the rifts in their clustering foliage peeps the softest and bluest and balmiest of skies. Duval, Monroe, Adams, Laura, Julia, Hogan, Ocean, Newnan, Market and Forsyth streets are particularly beautiful in this way.

Bay street can hardly be surpassed in the whole country as a promenade. It is the principal street in the city, and has many buildings which would do credit to communities of far greater pretensions. In the amount of business transacted by its merchants, and the general air and stir that is presented, it is surpassed by few in the country.

The curiosity and souvenir shops attract no small part of the stranger's attention. In the winter season these shops confront one every twenty steps during a walk through the city. They are full and running over with all sorts and kinds and shapes of Florida curiosities; alligator teeth polished to perfection, and worked into curious shapes for all curious uses; the stuffed birds and beasts and fish of Florida air and waters, and the live creatures as well; fans and plumes and screens and rare devices worked into form from the rich and radiant plumage of tropical birds, and, in fact, all the beautiful constructions that can be made from every Florida product, animate or inanimate, that lives or moves, or has its existence in the heavens above or the earth beneath, or in the waters under the earth, or in the deeps of the great sea. And back of these, and framed, as it were, in most of them, the smiling shopmen stand ready to exhibit or explain, or tempt to a speedy and extensive purchase.

Jacksonville has been called the "City of Hotels," and its superb hostelries are the wonder and delight of the pilgrim who comes to Florida, expecting to see an undeveloped country. It is safe to say that these splendid hotels have no superiors, and few equals. Anywhere among the elegant parlors and saloons, or upon the spacious balconies and verandas, may be seen costumes as handsome as the country affords, and the flash of diamonds is as dazzling here as at Saratoga or Cape May. In the course of the season at one of these hotels one will see as much style in dress and as many suggestions of unlimited wealth as at any American center of fashion. Each of the largest is provided

Take the SAVANNAH, FLORIDA & WESTERN RAILWAY,
The Thr ugh Car and Short Line to and from Florida.

The Leading Music House of Florida.

A. B. CAMPBELL,
Jacksonville, - - Florida.

PIANOS AND ORGANS.

BEST MAKES! LOWEST PRICES!! EASIEST TERMS!!!

PIANOS.	ORGANS.
KNABE,	WILCOX & WHITE,
WEBER,	CHICAGO COTTAGE,
HAINES BRO'S,	VOCALION.
MORRIS.	

All kinds of small Instruments at BED ROCK PRICES. Sheet Music at 25 to 50 per cent. below publisher's price.

Write or call for Catalogues, with full information as to Prices (cash and installments).

A. B. CAMPBELL,
JACKSONVILLE, FLA.

☞ Visit Green Cove Springs, a delightful Retreat for the Tourist, Invalid, Immigrant, or Sportsman. Excellent Hotels, the Borden Parks, Fine Fishing and Hunting. Reached by Steamer or Train.

with a special orchestra, and music and dancing make the gas-lit hours of the evening pass pleasanly away.

The more prominent hotels are the St. James, Windsor, Everett, Carleton, Placide, Duval, Tremont, Togni and Glenada, which are favorably known, not only in this but foreign countries, for their superior accommodations. It is safe to say that hotels which extend to the pleasure-seeker and invalid the many advantages offered by the hotels of Jacksonville do much to induce travel, and add to the pleasure of the visitors. There are also a large number of hotels of minor importance, suitable to persons of more limited means, which are conducted to please the most fastidious.

Large numbers make Jacksonville their headquarters for the season, making frequent excursions up the river and into the interior, but always returning with a sense of satisfaction and contentment. Society is cosmopolitan here to a marked degree, and is derived from all sections of this and foreign countries. Churches of all denominations, and the various shades of religious sentiment open their doors for the benefit of the devoutly disposed. As a place of sojourn for the tourist, the wealthy and fashionable classes, it is fast taking rank with Saratoga, Newport and Long Branch. With these elements it is becoming a necessity to pass a portion of each winter in Jacksonville. Here they meet the same associates that they found during the summer at the most noted Northern resorts, and there has simply been a change of climate and scenery. From the first of December to the middle of April the city is crowded to overflowing with guests from every State in the Union, and from the leading foreign countries. Here they find all the conditions requisite for an existence of ease, luxury and pleasure, and can set at defiance the bleak hills and icy breezes of their homes in the higher latitudes.

There are daily excursions to St. Augustine, Palatka, Fernandina, Mayport, Green Cove, and other favorite resorts, allowing abundance of time to inspect those localities.

Herein consists another attraction of this city; its proximity to the points above mentioned permits frequent visits that consume but little time, and cost but a trifle. The broad and noble St. Johns affords pastime for those fond of sailing or rowing. Safe and staunch boats are to be had in abundance, and furnish pleasure to those fond of such amusement. Steam ferry boats ply regularly to the opposite side of the river, where good roads, handsome residences, and thriving orange groves await inspection.

Take the SAVANNAH, FLORIDA & WESTERN RAILWAY,
The Through Car and Short Line to and from Florida.

JULIUS SALOMON,

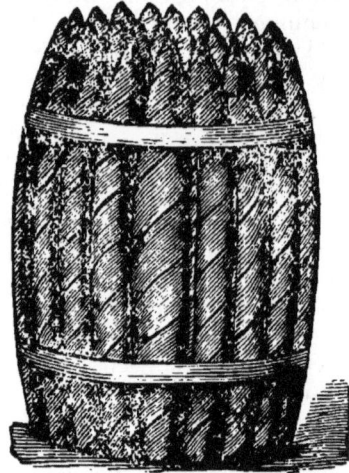

"El Rico" Brand of Cigars a Specialty.

Returns made Promptly.

Country Produce Solicited and

Wholesale Cigars, Tobaccos and Pipes,
67 West Bay Street, JACKSONVILLE, FLA.

THE DAILY TRIBUNE.

Daily $5.00 a Year.

Delivered by Carrier to any part of the City. Contains the complete local news of the City, with State and General News.

Weekly $1.00 a Year.

A Live Republican Paper.

SUBSCRIBE NOW.

D. C. DRAKE, Manager Tribune Publishing Co.,
Jacksonville, Fla.

☞ Visit Green Cove Springs, a delightful Retreat for the Tourist, Invalid, Immigrant or Sportsman. Excellent Hotels, the Borden Parks, Fine Fishing and Hunting. Reached by Steamer or Train.

This city is the base for supplies for a large portion of the State, and the facilities of the merchants are such that they are able to compete successfully with any other point.

There has been an appropriation made by the General Government for the erection of a public building, and a suitable location secured in the center of the city. Jacksonville is the site of the United States Court for the Northern District of Florida, and here are situated the offices of the Judge, Marshal and Clerk of that tribunal. The Collector of Internal Revenue for the State also has his headquarters in this city. Jacksonville also contains the largest and most important postoffice in the State, and is the distributing point for the bulk of the mails reaching Florida.

The Free Masons have lodges, chapters and encampments. The Odd Fellows are also in a flourishing condition. The Knights of Labor, Knights of Honor, Knights of Pythias, and Sons of Temperance are largely represented. St. Luke's Hospital, an institution sustained by private charity, affords relief to destitute invalids. The Library Association owns a handsome suite of rooms, where can be found the latest papers and magazines, and a collection of books.

Four daily papers, enterprising and well conducted, enjoy a large circulation. There are several journals that issue a weekly edition.

The public schools are large and convenient buildings, employing an excellent corps of teachers, and attended by large numbers of children. The facilities for obtaining an education are equally open to both races. The city is illuminated by gas and electric lights. Two clubs, the Yacht and the Jacksonville, have been formed for social enjoyment and intercourse, and contribute largely to the pleasure of their members and visitors.

There are three uniformed military companies, the Jacksonville Light Infantry, Metropolitan Light Infantry, and Light Artillery, and two companies of colored infantry.

Lines of steamers leave daily for Palatka, Sanford and all intermediate points on the St. Johns River, and to Mayport and Fort George Island, at the mouth of the same river. There is also a fine line of steamers (The Clyde) running direct to New York, carrying freight and passengers, which give the citizens of Jacksonville advantages possessed by no other portion of the State. Heavy freight is brought very cheap from northern points by the coasting vessels, constantly seeking the saw mills for cargoes of lumber.

Lines of street cars traverse the principal portions of the city, and reach out into the suburbs. East Jacksonville, Brook-

Take the **SAVANNAH, FLORIDA & WESTERN RAILWAY,**
The Through Car and Short Line to and from Florida.

HOME MARKET!

THE FLORIDA ORANGE AND VEGETABLE AUCTION COMPANY,

A. S. MANN, President and General Manager.

Sure and Quick Returns to the Grower.

The aim of the Auction Company is to concentrate the Orange and Vegetable crop in Jacksonville, and have the Northern Fruit Houses buy right here at home. The **GROWER DOES NOT TAKE ALL THE RISK OF TRANSPORTATION.**

This is the only house in the State which sells at Auction, and we sell no other way.

Starting in 1887 with no advocate but the manager, we have disarmed all enmity and criticism, and proved that **OUR SYSTEM IS NOT ONLY THE BEST,** but **THE ONLY ONE** which insures Large and Quick Returns to the Grower and Good Fruit to the Buyer.

Last year Growers selling through us the season round realized about $2.50 per box for their Oranges here in Jacksonville.

There are to-day represented in Jacksonville over one hundred of the best dealers in the Union, ready to buy at auction in case our growers will refuse to consign.

The Auction will open on the 20th day of November, 1890.

Send for Stencils and full Shipping Directions to the Office of the Company, or address P. O. Box "N." Jacksonville, Fla.

☞ Visit Green Cove Springs, a delightful Retreat for the Tourist, Invalid, Immigrant or Sportsman. Excellent Hotels, the Borden Parks, Fine Fishing and Hunting. Reached by Rail or Steamer.

lyn, LaVilla, Springfield, Oakland, Riverside and Campbellton are largely peopled by persons who do business in the city proper, but who have their residences in the thriving environs.

East Jacksonville contains large saw mills, employing numerous laborers, and furnishing immense quantities of lumber for home consumption and export. It is growing rapidly, and the roads leading out to the grounds of the Jockey Club Association, two miles distant from Jacksonville, are lined with handsome residences.

Brooklyn and Riverside are beautifully situated on a bold bluff overlooking the St. Johns River. Here are to be found most desirable sites for building purposes, many of which are already occupied by costly and imposing structures.

Springfield has been laid off in lots, and the sound of the hammer and saw are heard in every direction. The carpenters are also busy in LaVilla, Oakland and Campbellton, and the value of real estate is constantly on the increase in these thriving settlements. All contain churches, schools, thriving industries and beautiful homes.

The bulkheading of the river front and opening up of a new street is an important improvement of the near future.

That Jacksonville is a city with a glorious future none can dispute. The glory and beauty of its development will depend largely upon the enterprise and liberality of its people.

CITY CHURCHES.

Adventists—Corner Adams and First streets.
Tabernacle Baptist—West Church street, east of Julia.
Christian—Corner Beaver and Main streets.
Christian Memorial Chapel—Riverside.
First Congregational Church—Corner Hogan and Church streets.
Church of Good Shepherd—Brooklyn.
St. John's Episcopal—Corner Market and Duval.
St. Stephen's Episcopal—Corner Monroe and Third streets, LaVilla.
St. Andrew's Episcopal—Corner Brough and Duval streets.
Ahavath Chesed (Jewish)—Corner Laura and Union streets.
Church of St. John (Lutheran)—Corner Ashley and Laura streets.
St. Matthew's Methodist Episcopal—LaVilla.
St. Paul's Methodist Episcopal—Corner East Duval and Newnan streets.

Take the SAVANNAH, FLORIDA & WESTERN RAILWAY,
The Through Car and Short Line to and from Florida.

E. I. GORDON,

Successor to O. Z. Tyler & Co.,

FURNISHING UNDERTAKER

21 Newnan St., Jacksonville, Fla.

TELEPHONE CALL 121.

Orders by Telephone at all hours of Day or Night promptly executed.

ESTABLISHED 1876.   TELEPHONE 241.

A. CAMPBELL,

Wholesale and Retail Dealer in all Kinds of

NORTHERN MEATS, GAME AND POULTRY.

Proprietor of the Jacksonville Steam Sausage Factory.

Kettle Rendered Lard and Tallow a Specialty,

Office Nos. 2 and 37 Old City Market,

Jacksonville, Florida.

☞ Visit Green Cove Springs, a delightful Retreat for the Tourist, Invalid, Immigrant or Sportsman. Excellent Hotels, the Borden Parks, Fine Fishing and Hunting. Reached by Steamer or Train.

Trinity M. E.—Opposite City Park, West Monroe street.
Presbyterian—Corner Newnan and Monroe streets.
Roman Catholic—Corner Newnan and Church streets.

PUBLIC BUILDINGS AND PLACES OF AMUSEMENT.

Sub-Tropical—Main street, corner First street.
Court House—Market street, corner Forsyth.
County Jail—Liberty street, corner Beaver.
Postoffice—Mohawk Block, East Bay street.
Mayor's Court—Ocean street.
Jacksonville Water Works—Main street.
U. S. Signal Service Office—Astor Block.
Park Theatre—Opposite St. James Hotel, corner Laura and Duval streets.
Telegraph Office—Hubbard Block, Main street.
Express Office—Astor Block, corner Bay and Hogan streets.
Home for the Friendless—Evergreen street.
The Orphanage—Ocean street, corner Duval
St. Luke's Hospital—Monroe street, corner Palmetto.

SOCIETY ORGANIZATIONS.

O. M. Mitchell Post G. A. R.—Postoffice Building.
Florida Camp, No. 1, C. Vet.—Corner Adams and Laura streets.
Brotherhood of Locomotive Engineers, No. 26.
Hebrew Benevolent Society.
Irish Land League—Corner Adams and Laura streets.
Jacksonvile Typographical Union, No. 162.
Mechanics' Steam Fire Engine Company—Adams street.
The Scottish Association of Florida—No. 20½ West Bay.
Woman's Exchange—Corner Forsyth and Market streets.
Y. M. C. A.—Laura street, between Forsyth and Adams.
Duval Lodge, No. 18 (Masonic)—Bay and Market streets.
Solomon Lodge, No. 20 (Masonic)—Bay and Market streets.
Florida Lodge, No. 1, I. O. O. F.—No. 44 Market street.
Montefiore, No. 2, K. of P.—Reed's Block, Bay street.
S. S. Davis, No. 15, K. of P.—National Bank State of Florida building, Bay street.
Jacksonville Council, No. 888, A. L. H.—Bay and Main streets.
Knights of the Golden Eagle—S. S. Davis, K. of P., Hall.
Fidelity Lodge, No. 2, A. O. U. W.—No. 52½ West Bay street.

Take the SAVANNAH, FLORIDA & WESTERN RAILWAY,
The Through Car and Short Line to and from Florida.

GAINESVILLE.

Gainesville is the county site of Alachua county, Florida, and has the finest court house in the State. The town is advantageously located. Being the centre of one of the best vegetable growing, and farming districts in the State, more vegetables, such as cucumbers, tomatoes, Irish and sweet potatoes, cabbage, beans and strawberries are shipped to the Northern market than from any other point in the State. The lands in this vicinity also produce profitable crops of cotton, corn, oats, hay, sugar cane, rice and fine grades of tobacco. Some of the finest brands of long staple, Sea Island, cotton being produced in this county. The growing of Havana tobacco, as far as tried, has proved very profitable.

Gainesville is situated in the famous phosphate belt, and cannot but be very much benefited by the development of that important industry.

The city contains between four and five thousand inhabitants, is well supplied with churches, both white and colored. Some of the best church edifices in the State are found here.

Its educational facilities cannot be excelled in the State, it being the seat of the East Florida Seminary, a State military institution and one of the best managed schools in the State. It also has an excellent graded public school and good private schools for white, and an excellent graded public school for colored children. It has also been selected as the site of a large Manual Training and Normal Institute for the colored youth of both sexes.

The city is well supplied with hotels for the accommodation of the traveling public. The Brown House and the St. Nicholas being the best.

Transportation facilities are supplied by the S., F. & W., the F. C. & P. and Florida Southern R. R., and is excellent. Several roads are projected, some are under contract and the others will doubtless be built. Among the projected lines is the Gainesville, Tallahassee and Western. Gainesville and Brunswick, and extension of the S., F. & W. to South Florida.

At this point is located one of the most extensive cotton ginnery establishments and largest furniture factory in the State. Besides, it has moss mills, fertilizer and ice factories, sash, door, blind and wood working establishments. The streets are well paved with rock and shaded with beautiful live and water oaks. The city contains the largest and best court house, is the seat of the United States land office, has two banks, quite a number of fine business blocks and some as extensive stocks of goods as are found anywhere in the State.

CHAPIN & MELRATH,
GAINESVILLE, FLA.,
REAL ESTATE AND COLLECTION AGENTS.

Lands for sale in lots from ten to twenty thousand acres in any and all sections of the State, at prices ranging from one to ten dollars per acre.

☞ Visit Green Cove Springs, a delightful Retreat for the Tourist, Invalid, Immigrant or Sportsman. Excellent Hotels, the Borden Parks, Fine Fishing and Hunting. Reached by Steamer or Train.

Duval Division S. of T.—No. 48½ West Bay street.
Guiding Star, No. 98, S. of T.—Nellie street, East Jacksonville.
W. C. T. U.—No. 4½ Ocean street.
Florida Yacht Club—Foot of Market street.
Jacksonville Gun Club.

HOTELS.

Acme Hotel—111 West Bay street.
Bettelini's Hotel—No. 16 East Bay street.
Carleton House—Corner Bay and Market streets.
Central House—No. 49 West Forsyth street.
Duval Hotel—Corner Forsyth and Hogan streets.
Everett Hotel—Corner Forsyth and Julia streets.
Glenada Hotel—No. 118 West Church street.
Clifton Hotel—Corner Forsyth and Cedar streets.
Grand View Hotel—Forsyth street, between Bridge and Clay streets.
Hotel Roseland—Shell road, opposite Eighth Avenue, Fairfield.
Hotel Togni—Corner Bay and Newnan streets.
Johnson House—No. 94 West Adams street.
LaFayette House—Forsyth street, near Main.
Oxford Hotel—No. 90 Laura street.
Placide—Main street, between Forsyth and Adams.
St. Charles Hotel—No. 80 West Forsyth street.
St. James Hotel—Duval street, between Laura and Hogan.
St. Johns House—No. 41 West Forsyth street.
The Chelsea—No. 63 Main street.
Warner House—No. 143 Laura street.
Windsor Hotel—Corner Hogan and Monroe streets.
Travelers' Hotel—Corner Bay and Cedar streets.

BUSINESS BLOCKS AND HALLS.

Abell Block—Nos. 32, 34 and 36 West Bay street.
Army of the Republic Hall—Corner Bay and Laura streets.
Astor Block—Corner Bay and Hogan streets.
Atlantic Block—Nos. 26 and 28 West Bay street.
Bostwick Block—Corner Bay and Main streets.
Burbridge Block—Corner Main and Forsyth streets.
City Hall—Foot of Market street.
Ely Block—Corner Forsyth and Laura streets.
Everett Hotel Block—Corner Bay and Julia streets.
Freedman's Bank Building—Corner Main and Forsyth streets.

Take the SAVANNAH, FLORIDA & WESTERN RAILWAY,
The Through Car and Short Line to and from Florida.

GILBERT,

CENTENNIAL MEDAL, PHILADELPHIA, 1876.

STATE MEDAL, NEW JERSEY, 1878.

MEDAL AMERICAN INSTITUTE, NEW YORK, 1877.

FIRST PREMIUM, STATE AND COUNTY FAIR, JACKSONVILLE, FLA.

THE JEWELER,
Watchmaker and Optician.

ESTABLISHED IN JACKSONVILLE 1868.

HEADQUARTERS FOR

FINE GOLD AND SILVER WATCHES,
CHAINS, CHARMS, SCARF PINS,
SLEEVE BUTTONS, FINGER RINGS, Etc.

THE BEST GOODS AT THE VERY LOWEST PRICES.

Fine Watch and Chronometer Repairing a Specialty.

After an experience of over thirty-five years, I feel confident that I can give entire satisfaction. All work warranted.

E. F. GILBERT,
13 East Bay St.,   Jacksonville, Fla.

☞ Visit Green Cove Springs, a delightful Retreat for the Tourist, Invalid, Immigrant or Sportsman. Excellent Hotels, the Borden Parks, Fine Fishing and Hunting. Reached by Steamer or Train.

Hazeltine Block—Corner Bay and Laura streets.
Herkimer Block—Corner Bay and Newnan streets.
Holmes Block—Nos. 99 and 105 West Bay street.
Holmes (new) Block—Nos. 48, 50 and 52 West Bay street.
Hubbard Block—Corner Main and Forsyth streets.
Hudnall's Building—Nos. 43 and 45 West Forsyth street.
L'Engle Block—Corner Main and Adams street.
Law Building—No. 44 East Forsyth street.
Law Exchange—Corner Market and Forsyth streets.
Lincoln Hall—Second street, LaVilla.
McConihe Block—Nos. 58, 40 and 42 West Bay street.
McCormick's Hall—Washington street.
Masonic Hall—Mohawk Block, corner Bay and Market streets.
Masonic Temple—Corner Julia and Orange streets.
Metropolitan Hall—No. 17 East Bay street.
Mohawk Block—Corner Bay and Market streets.
Mason's Block—Corner Bay and Julia streets.
Meyer & Muller Block—Corner Bay and Liberty streets.
Smith Block—Forsyth street, between Main and Ocean.

INTERESTING ITEMS.

Population, 25,000; number of manufacturing industries, seventy-six, classified as follows: Iron and brass work foundries, four; bridge builders, one; artificial stone, one; saw and planing mills, eight; shingle mill, one; gas works, one; electric light works, one; palmetto fiber factory, one; marble yards, two; brick yards, two; boat builders, two; blank book manufactories, three; grist mills, two; ice factories, two; cabinet makers, two; manufacturing confectioners, four; carriage and wagon factories, seven; chemical laboratories, two; cigar factories, fourteen; cigar box factories, one; bottling works, three; coffee and spice mills, one; fertilizer and phosphate works, one; soap and fertilizer factories, three; manufactories of curiosities, four; marine railways, two; harness and saddle factory, one; trunk factory, one. The total amount of capital invested in these various industries is $1,400,800. The annual product is over $1,000,000.

The number of public buildings is six, costing (including the amount to be expended on the Government building) $458,000.

Number of school buildings, ten, costing $56,000.

Number of churches (including all denominations), forty; white, eighteen; colored, twenty-two; value of public library property, $20,000; number of volumes contained in library, 3,500.

Take the SAVANNAH, FLORIDA & WESTERN RAILWAY,
The Through Car and Short Line to and from Florida.

THE EVERETT,

Jacksonville's Largest and Finest Hotel. Built of Brick and Stone.

Now under the management of McIVER & BAKER, formerly of the Duval.
RATE $3.00 AND $4.00 PER DAY.

L. CAMERON,

GARDEN, FIELD

——— AND ———

FLOWER SEEDS,

23 EAST BAY ST.,

Jacksonville, Florida.

☞ Visit Green Cove Springs, a delightful Retreat for the Tourist, Invalid, Immigrant or Sportsman. Excellent Hotels, the Borden Parks, Fine Fishing and Hunting. Reached by Steamer or Train.

Twenty railroads, operating 2,448 miles; two lines of ocean steamers; six lines of river steamers.

Three artesian wells, having a flow of 4,737,172 gallons of water every twenty-four hours. Nine miles of sewers through pipes from eight to twenty-four inches in diameter. Two lines of street railroads, covering eleven miles of streets; motive power, horses and mules. A paid Fire Department, employing twenty-six men; annual expense of Fire Department, $13,200; the Gamewell fire alarm system is used. The Police Department consists of thirty-one men; annual expense of the department, $21,000. The city tax rate per $100 is $1.62½. Assessed valuation of city property, $12,335,000. City government: Governed by a board of eighteen Councilmen appointed by the Governor of the State. The City Council elects the Mayor and all other municipal officers.

The City of St. Augustine.

NOW put on thy musty garments, oh, St. Augustine! Gather the cobwebs around thy ancient ruins. Lay out the speaking emblems of thy antiquity; for the time of the year is come when the people gather from near and from far to see the patriarch of cities with a Ponce de Leon flowing in its heart! Who that has traveled southward has not seen St. Augustine? Who has not stood amid the venerable memories of that old cathedral whose masses have been chanted by Spanish priest or hooded monk or modern prelate for more than three centuries of time? Who has not gazed in speculative retrospection upon the cabalistic Spanish inscribed upon the monument of the plaza de la Constitucion? Who has not loved to pace that matchless sea-wall promenade swept by the freshest of Atlantic breezes and kissed along its lovely length by the plashing wavelets that have dashed themselves in sterner form against it for a hundred years in vain? And who, amid the crowding memories and vivid antiquities of old Fort Marion, has not caught the glow of chivalry from the old Castilian days of Spain? It is no wonder that St. Augustine has been growing in popularity year by year, until the last season crowded all the hotels, filled the boarding houses and private homes with tourists, and left many barred of entrance by the impossibility of accommodation.

Take the **SAVANNAH, FLORIDA & WESTERN RAILWAY,**
The Through Car and Short Line to and from Florida.

JOHN H. FOWLER,
Plumbing, Tinning,
Steam and Gas Fitting.

Shop in Rear of Store, 40 and 42 East Bay St.

TELEPHONE 148.

JACKSONVILLE, - - FLORIDA.

FULL LINE OF

BATH TUBS, PUMPS, PIPE, Etc.

STEAMBOAT WORK A SPECIALTY.

CHARLES O. OTIS,
Cor. Maine (Pine) and Adams Streets,
RETAIL DEALER IN
FOREIGN AND DOMESTIC
Cigars and Tobacco
Full Line of Oranges. Fine Fruits, Confectionery, Etc.

OWEN TRAVERS,
WEST END SAMPLE ROOMS.

WHOLESALE AND RETAIL DEALER IN

Imported and Domestic Liquors, Wines and Cigars,

93 WEST BAY ST., - - - JACKSONVILLE, FLA.

☞ Visit Green Cove Springs, a delightful Retreat for the Tourist, Invalid, Immigrant or Sportsman. Excellent Hotels, the Borden Parks, Fine Fishing and Hunting. Reached by Steamer and Train.

The city is located on a peninsula formed by the San Sebastian and Matanzas rivers, and is built in the form of a parallogram a mile in length and three-quarters of a mile wide. It contains about 10,000 inhabitants, but during the winter season the population is much larger, owing to its wonderful popularity as a resort, which is yearly increasing. As the stranger wanders through the shady streets, hundreds of rare and interesting sights may be found on every side. Among the principal points of interest to the tourist we might mention

FORT MARION,

formerly called San Marco, and anciently San Juan de Pinos, covers four acres, and commands the harbor and its entrance from the sea. It is built of coquina; its walls are twenty-one feet high and twelve feet thick. It has four bastions, and in all respects is a military castle. It has twenty-seven casements thirty-five feet long and eighteen feet wide, and its complement is one hundred guns and one thousand men. (See Chapin's Hand Book of St. Augustine for a full history of this famous old fortress and a full account of the finding of the mysterious cage, which was broken up by the St. Augustine blacksmith for the use of the iron of which it was composed. The skeleton found in the cage was buried outside the fort, and, it is said, was afterward exhumed and deposited in the St. Augustine Museum, where many other Spanish relics may now be seen.)

THE SEA WALL

was built by the United States government, 1837–43, at an expense of $100,000, to protect the city from the encroachment of the sea. It rises ten feet above high-water mark, and the capping of granite is just wide enough for two persons to walk abreast. The United States Barracks, at the Southern extremity of the sea wall, are now occupied by United States troops. Prior to 1586, the Franciscan monks established a convent here, hence the walls of this structure may now be three centuries old.

THE CITY GATES.

Two picturesque square pillars of coquina, surmounted with Moorish capitals, bearing marks of great antiquity, stand at the head of St. George Street, within a gun shot of the Museum. When, or by whom, these strange pillars were erected, no one knows, but they furnish ample scope for the speculation of the antiquarian.

THE OLD SPANISH RELICS,

of which so much is said, are deposited in the Museum, and should be seen by every visitor.

Take the SAVANNAH, FLORIDA & WESTERN RAILWAY,
The Through Car and Short Line to and from Florida.

ESTIMATES ON SHORT NOTICE.

J. MARZYCK.   W. H. BROWNE.

J. MARZYCK & CO.,
CONTRACTORS,

BALDWIN BLOCK, - - - JACKSONVILLE, FLA.

RAILROADS, CANALS, BRIDGES,
DOCKS, WHARVES, MILLS, DREDGES,
FOUNDATIONS, LIGHTERS,
TRESTLES, WAREHOUSES, DEPOTS.

JOHN C. KERNAN,
ARCHITECT AND BUILDER,
Office, No. 56 East Ashley St.,
JACKSONVILLE, · FLA.

☞ Visit Green Cove Springs, a delightful Retreat for the Tourist, Invalid, Immigrant or Sportsman. Excellent Hotels, the Borden Parks, Fine Fishing and Hunting. Reached by Steamer or Train.

THE CATHEDRAL.

This antiquated Catholic church was built in 1793, at a cost of $16,650, and stands on the north side of the Plaza. The Moorish belfry contains a chime of four bells placed on four several niches, three of which form a horizontal line across the tower, and the other is above; these, together with the clock below, are so arranged as to form a perfect cross. One of these bells, supposed to be the oldest in the country, bears the inscription: "Sancte Joseph, ora pro nobis, D. 1689." Which, translated, means, "Holy Joseph, pray for us. Dedicated 1689." This bell is supposed to have belonged to the earlier Church.

CEMETERIES.

The Huguenot Cemetery, near the city gates; the Catholic Cemetery, west of Spanish Street; and the Military Cemetery, which contains the graves of General Dade and his soldiers.

THE LIGHTHOUSE,

on Anastasia Island, which is 164 feet high, was built in 1873, at a cost upwards of $100,000. The lantern cost $16,000. The visitor will be well repaid for ascending the steps by the enjoyment of the magnificent view. Near by, on the east side of the island, are the ruins of the old Spanish lighthouse, erected during the Seventeenth Century, which was destroyed by a furious storm, June 20, 1880.

THE PLAZA,

containing the Spanish monument, erected in 1812, to commemorate the Spanish Liberal Constitution.

There are also a number of large and costly churches, the old market, the United States Barracks, the north beach, noted for the quantity of beautiful sea shells exposed at low tide. Scores of walks and drives will not tell half the delightful story of St. Augustine's wealth of the quaint, curious and beautiful. Her hotels are equal to those of any winter resort in the world, the mammoth Ponce de Leon taking front rank as being the most costly, the largest, and most unique and magnificently appointed hotel in America. To see the Ponce de Leon is alone worth a long and dusty tramp amid difficulties which can never be encountered by a Florida tourist. Reader, if you have never visited St. Augustine, you are putting off until some more convenient time one of the pleasures of a life-time.

Take the **SAVANNAH, FLORIDA & WESTERN RAILWAY,**
The Through Car and Short Line to and from Florida.

ATTENTION!

Our Store is now open to supply the public with the following goods
AT CLOSE PRICES:

CROCKERY, HARDWARE, TINWARE, WOODENWARE, WILLOWWARE,

And All the Latest Novelties.

REICHARD & QUACKENBUSCH,
151 West Bay, Next Door to Travelers.

The Jacksonville Auction and Commission House of

JULIUS SLAGER & CO.,
DEALERS IN ALL KINDS OF GOODS.

Diamonds, Watches and Jewelry a Specialty.

WHOLESALE DEALERS IN ALL KINDS OF SILVER SHOW-CASES.

32 West Bay Street,   -   -   JACKSONVILLE, FLA.

Special attention paid to Out-Door Auction Sales of Real Estate, Live Stock, Furniture, and all kinds of Merchandise. Money advanced on personal property.

ALL ABOUT FLORIDA.

FLORIDA DISPATCH, FARMER AND FRUIT GROWER AND FARMERS' ALLIANCE.

Three Leading Papers United into One. A 24-Page Illustrated Paper of Unsurpassed Excellence. Established in 1869.

LEADING AGRICULTURAL AND HORTICULTURAL PAPER IN THE GULF STATES.

BEST ADVERTISING MEDIUM IN THE STATE.

Each issue contains detailed and descriptive information about the State and the resources and advantages of its several sections; also classified departments on practical Farming, Gardening, Fruit Growing, Stock Raising, Poultry Keeping, and kindred interests in the State. A department on home life and home making in Florida, and other matters of interest to all whose attention is turned Southward.

LOOK AT OUR PREMIUMS:

Fifteen Volumes Chas. Dickens' or Walter Scott's Novels, nicely bound, and our paper, for $3. The premiums are worth three times the price charged for books and newspaper.

Subscription $2 per Year. On Trial for Three Months, 50 cents.
SPECIMEN COPIES FREE.

CHAS. W. DaCOSTA,

JACKSONVILLE, FLA.,   -   -   -   -   PUBLISHER.

☞ Visit Green Cove Springs, a delightful Retreat for the Tourist, Invalid, Immigrant or Sportsman. Excellent Hotels, the Borden Parks, Fine Fishing and Hunting. Reached by Steamer or Train.

The City of Fernandina.

FERNANDINA is a little over an hour's ride from Jacksonville, by the Florida Central and Peninsular train, and is the county seat of Nassau County. The city was founded by the Spaniards in the year 1632, and has a population of about 3,000, largely increased during the winter season. It has an important trade in lumber, possesses a large cotton ginning establishment, a manufactory of cotton-seed oil, one of the best hotels in the South, a large number of fine residences, business houses and churches. Near the city may be found a large number of sugar, cotton and orange plantations. The climate is very mild and healthy. It has the largest and deepest harbor on the eastern coast of the State. It is beautifully located in a sheltered situation on the west side of Amelia Island, the northern extremity of which guards the entrance to Cumberland Sound and the extensive land-locked harbor, into which open the St. Marys River, and Amelia River from Nassau Inlet.

One of the chief attractions of Fernandina is the Amelia Beach, a noble stretch of smooth, shining sand, sloping gently from the foot of the great "sand-dune" which lies along the outer edge of the island far out under the shallow waters of the Atlantic, and extending from one end of the island to the other, a distance of over twenty miles. The surface of the sand at the edge of the water is as hard as a floor, forming a magnificent drive, and a firm, hard shell road extends from the city to the beach, a distance of nearly two miles.

Connection is made at Fernandina, semi-weekly, with the elegant steamships of the Clyde Line and Mallory Line to and from Charleston and New York; with the Sea Island Route steamers to and from Savannah, Tuesday and Friday, and daily with the Cumberland Route, daily to and from Brunswick, Macon, Atlanta, Chattanooga, and all points West and Northwest.

A branch track from the city to the beach has recently been completed, rendering the facilities for reaching this notable resort perfect.

Eight miles from Fernandina, by water, on Cumberland Island, is the famous estate of Dungeness, several thousand acres in extent, bestowed by the State of Georgia upon General Nathaniel Green, and belonging for many years to his descendants.

Take the **SAVANNAH, FLORIDA & WESTERN RAILWAY,**
The Through Car and Short Line to and from Florida.

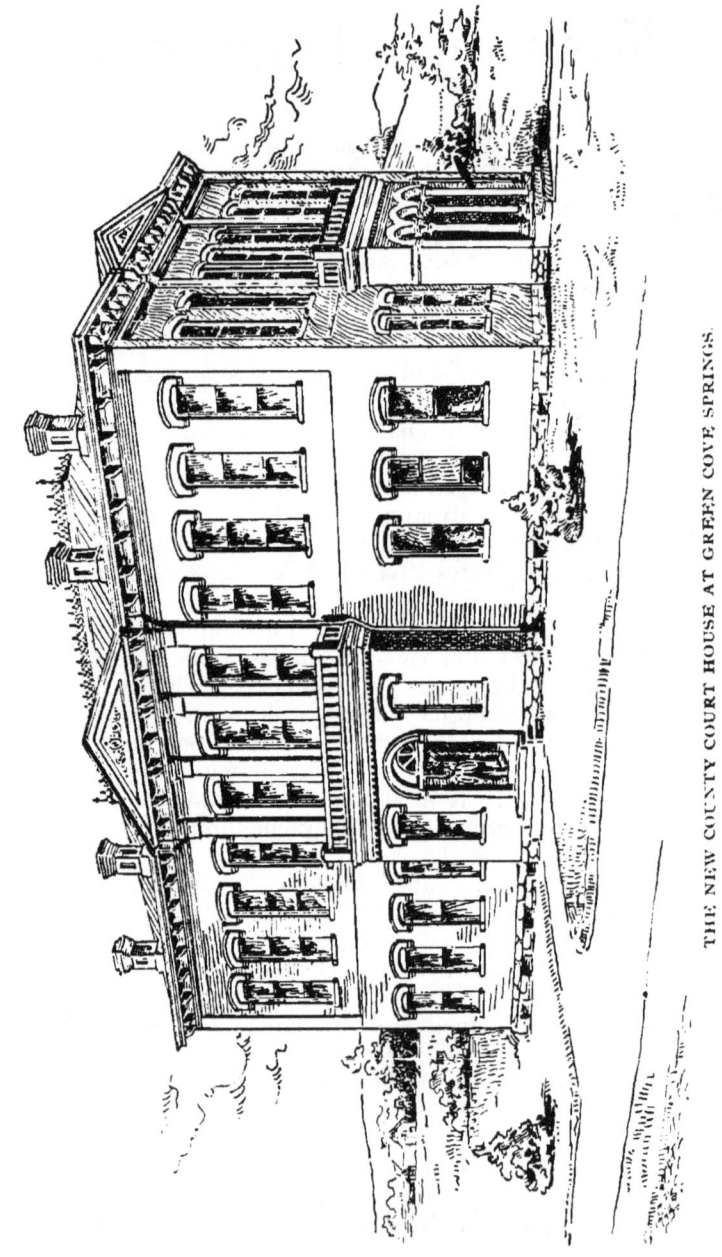

THE NEW COUNTY COURT HOUSE AT GREEN COVE SPRINGS.

☛ Visit Green Cove Springs, a delightful Retreat for the Tourist, Invalid, Immigrant, or Sportsman. Excellent Hotels, the Borden Parks, Fine Fishing and Hunting. Reached by Steamer or Train.

Broad avenues, bounded by plantations of ancient orange and olive trees, and bordered by giant oaks, stretch grandly away on either side of the homestead. The old family burying-ground, with its ancient tombs (one of which covers the mortal part of the renowned soldier known to fame and the history of this country as "Light-Horse Harry" Lee), is located in a grove not far from the mansion.

Green Cove Springs.
(THE PARLOR CITY.)

EVERYBODY has heard of Green Cove Springs, the most enterprising and beautiful little city on the noble St. Johns. Proud of its present and with a fixed faith in its future, Green Cove Springs enjoys an enviable and not unpleasant self-satisfaction which vents itself in municipal and speculative enterprise. The location of the town is very attractive, circling about a wooded and picturesque hollow, from which gushes a bold, magnificent sulphur spring, with a basin as large as the foundation of a cottage, and as deep in places as the cottage's peaked roof. Three thousand gallons of water per minute, clear and pure as crystal, gush from the great cavernous boil. The water is strong sulphur and is esteemed a very fine remedial agent in cases of neuralgia, nervous prostration, rheumatism, liver and kidney complaints. The water empties from the spring into several bathing pools of unusual size and beauty, which are open and in use all the year round.

Think of open air bathing in December. It is the county seat and one of the most famous and delightful winter resorts in Florida.

Its resident population is rapidly increasing, and will soon reach the 5,000 mark.

As the visitor wanders through the shady streets of the town, he can be but favorably impressed with the neat and tidy appearance of all he sees; miles of good sidewalks, beautiful parks, mammoth hotels, commodius churches, schools, pretty residences, and lovely flower gardens, stately oaks and magnolias, draped in Spanish moss, with a background of magnificent pine woods, make a scene where one could rest for hours

"And come and come again,
That he might call it up when far away."

Take the SAVANNAH, FLORIDA & WESTERN RAILWAY,
The Through Car and Short Line to and from Florida.

✳ ✳ BORDEN'S ✳ ✳

Clay County Wood-Working Company.

LUMBER

Of Every Description, in any Quantity or Quality.

PRICES ALWAYS REASONABLE.

For information, call on or address,

BORDEN'S CLAY COUNTY WOOD-WORKING COMPANY,

GREEN COVE SPRINGS, CLAY COUNTY, FLA.

Borden's Wharf,

FOOT OF WALNUT ST.,

GREEN COVE SPRINGS, FLORIDA.

General Depot for all the Boats on the River.

Waiting Rooms for Ladies and Gentlemen.

LARGE STORAGE ROOMS FOR FREIGHT.

TICKET OFFICE: W. E. COLEMAN, Agent.

☞ Visit Green Cove Springs, a delightful Retreat for the Tourist, Invalid, Immigrant or Sportsman. Excellent Hotels, the Borden Parks, Fine Fishing and Hunting. Reached by Rail or Steamer.

The transportation facilities are unsurpassed in any town in Florida; three large piers, jutting out in the St. Johns, afford convenient access to sea-going vessels and river craft of every kind, while the Jascksonville, Tampa & Key West Railroad, running through the center of the town, gives communication with the railroad systems of the country. Through some of the principal streets of the town a line of street railroad has been completed, and is now in operation, connecting with all the railroad stations, wharves and hotels. There are also two lines of steamers, the Beach and Miller line, running daily boats, and the New Independent Line, making daily trips between Green Cove Springs and Jacksonville.

In all this broad land of ours, there is no nobler trip than a sail up the great tropical river from Jacksonville to Green Cove Springs. The entire distance of thirty miles is as beautiful as a dream. When you round Grassy Point off Jacksonville, your throbbing steamer seeks the center of a great stream, whose average width is three miles, widening at Green Cove Springs to five.

Such a world of waters; sometimes stretching for miles in a straight, majestic sweep, and then turning slowly, as becomes its size and greatness, in a long stately curve that makes a bay or cove large enough for a nation's navy to lie at bay. The never-ceasing sea breeze ruffles the broad surface into waves that break into white caps as merrily, if not as noisily, as the billows of the great ocean. There is a feeling of awe, the majesty of size, the grandeur of scope, and the sublimity of power in this mighty stream on which your steamer rides like a tiny thing at the mercy of the river god.

The great river seems indeed a chain of lakes, throbbing with ocean tides and inheriting the swell of ocean waves. Along the circumscribing shores that bind its mighty current, the succession of fair cities, of thrifty towns, of orange groves and grand hotels, is strikingly beautiful. The shores so far away grow shapely and regular in perspective, and die away in walls of green against the horizon. Mandarin's bright groves first greet the traveler's eye, followed quickly by the tasteful pier and snowy fences over which peeps the green of Orange Park. Magnolia looms in stately beauty from its crest of emerald sward; and Green Cove's fair canon with its healing spring makes a sweet picture in the semi-circle of the river's sweep long to be remembered. Reader, if you doubt God's goodness and power and want to become a better man or woman, the delight-

Take the SAVANNAH, FLORIDA & WESTERN RAILWAY,
The Through Car and Short Line to and from Florida.

Florida Real Estate.

J. E. LOW,
Green Cove Springs, Florida.

UNIMPROVED LANDS IN HEAVY BLOCKS,
ORANGE GROVES, CITY PROPERTY,
RAILROAD LANDS.

Taxes Paid for Non-Residents.

SIDNEY F. HANFORD,
GREEN COVE SPRINGS, FLORIDA.

REAL ESTATE

BOUGHT, SOLD AND EXCHANGED.

LOANS NEGOTIATED.   ABSTRACTS FURNISHED.
COLLECTION OF TAXES AND ALL GENERAL BUSINESS
PROMPTLY ATTENDED TO.

ADDRESS,

SYDNEY F. HANFORD,
Clerk of Circuit Court, Green Cove Springs, Clay County, Florida.

ESTABLISHED 1890.

The Spring.

OFFICIAL NEWSPAPER OF CLAY COUNTY.

Published at the Celebrated Watering Place and Resort,
GREEN COVE SPRINGS, FLA.
CIRCULATED LARGELY LOCALLY AND ABROAD.

W. D. RANDALL,
Editor and Manager.

☞ Visit Green Cove Springs, a delightful Retreat for the Tourist, Invalid, Immigrant or Sportsman. Excellent Hotels, the Borden Parks, Fine Fishing and Hunting. Reached by Steamer or Train.

ful two hours spent on the St. Johns river in reaching Green Cove Springs, will prove a sweet blessing indeed.

The bathing and fishing at Green Cove Springs is unsurpassed, black bass and speckled bream are caught in large numbers. Quail are abundant, and the numerous deer and turkey in the neighboring forests contribute much to the lover of rod and gun.

Among its numerous attractions is St. David's Path, or the Lover's Walk, where one may wander over little hills, through miniature dell, sparkling rivulets, in and out among magnificent moss-laden oaks, the sweet scented Magnolia, and amid flowers which fill the air with fragrance.

Florida has numerous attractions, but none are more worthy of special mention than Marion Borden Park, the most beautiful spot in the South. Not only is it celebrated far and wide for its great beauty, but stands as an everlasting monument to one of Florida's most public spirited citizens, enterprising and generous in every movement which tends to advance the interests of his town, county or State, as well as to increase the dimples of joy in the homes of the needy and afflicted.

The immense tract of land purchased by Hon. John G. Borden, of which Marion Borden Park is a part, has been layed out in parks, courts, drives, circles, and avenues in a most striking manner, and when completed will present a scene as near Eden as we may ever hope to behold below.

The hotels of Green Cove Springs are models of comfort, overlooking the river and furnished with all modern conveniences for the accomodation of their numerous guests. There are also a large number of excellent boarding houses where board may be obtained at reasonable prices.

There are a large number of secret societies, a splendid newspaper, "The Green Cove Spring," express, telephone and telegraph offices, and daily mails, the new county court house, amusement halls, the Ladies' Villiage Improvement Association, an admirable society of ladies, whose chief aim is to maintain for the city the reputation of being the neatest and sweetest community in the State. Their work is well done and an example set which towns of far greater pretensions would do well to follow.

There are also a number of large manufacturing plants, among which we notice Borden's Clay County Wood-Working Co., the car works of Blain Bros. and the Clay County Brick Works.

The rapid increase in population and the vast and wonderful improvements now going on, tell the story of the city's future in words more forcible than we can employ.

Take the SAVANNAH, FLORIDA & WESTERN RAILWAY,
The Through Car and Short Line to and from Florida.

OWN A HOME?

Which you can leave for your family in case of death?

STOP PAYING RENT

and enrich yourself instead of some landlord?

PAY OFF A MORTGAGE

which works when you are asleep?

Receive Large Profits

on your investment?

SAVE MONEY?

If so, call on or address the

Home Investment Building and Loan Association,

34 LAURA ST., JACKSONVILLE, FLA.

Authorized Capital, $1,000,000.   Paid Up Capital Nov. 1st, $93,335.16.

DO YOU WANT TO

☞ Visit Green Cove Springs, a delightful Retreat for the Tourist, Invalid, Immigrant, or Sportsman. Excellent Hotels, the Borden Parks, Fine Fishing and Hunting. Reached by Steamer or Train.

The City of Palatka.

THE thriving and picturesque city of Palatka is located on the St. Johns River, seventy-five miles from Jacksonville by boat and fifty-six miles by the Jacksonville, Tampa and Key West Railway. The town is situated on an inlet, or cove, and forms a splendid fishing, boating and bathing ground. Previous to the year 1837, the town was occupied by the Indians. It is the largest town above Jacksonville on the river, and boasts of a population of 5,000. Palatka is the county seat of Putnam County, and an important railroad center and distributing point for lumber and vegetables. Her telegraph and postal communications are excellent. Beautiful residences, commodious churches, good schools, magnificent hotels and business blocks speak volumes for the enterprise and public spirit of the citizens. The climate is especially beneficial to those suffering with pulmonary complaints. Among the amusements of Palatka boating, yachting, fishing and hunting have a prominent place. Some of the finest orange groves in the State are located near the city, and should receive a visit from the traveler, who seeks the beauties of our sunny clime.

POSTOFFICES IN THE STATE OF FLORIDA.

ESTABLISHED UP TO JANUARY 1, 1889.

Abbott	Ankona	Auburndale
Aberdeen	Anona	Aucilla
Acron	Anthony	Aurantia
Add	Apalachicola	Averill
Alachua	Apopka	Avon Park
Alafia	Arcadia	Bagdad
Alamo	Archer	Baker's Mill
Alpine	Argo	Baldwin
Altamont	Argyle	Banana
Altamonte Springs	Arlington	Bannerville
Alto	Armour	Barberville
Altoona	Armstrong	Barco
Alva	Arredonda	Barkers
Anastasia	Astabula	Bartow
Anclote	Astor	Bascom

Take the SAVANNAH, FLORIDA & WESTERN RAILWAY,
The Through Car and Short Line to and from Florida.

ONCE A CUSTOMER, ALWAYS A CUSTOMER.

FINE GOODS.   LOW PRICES.

THE FLORIDA TEAPOT.

THOS. P. BRENNAN,

DEALER IN

CHOICE FANCY

AND

FAMILY GROCERIES,

RICH OLD WINES AND LIQUORS,

CIGARS AND TOBACCO.

TRY OUR TEAS AND COFFEES.

USE BRENNAN'S PROSPERITY PATENT FLOUR.

NO. 72 WEST BAY STREET.

PROMPT ATTENTION.   FREE DELIVERY.

☞ Visit Green Cove Springs, a delightful Retreat for the Tourist, Invalid, Immigrant or Sportsman. Excellent Hotels, the Borden Parks, Fine Fishing and Hunting. Reached by Steamer and Train.

Bayard	Campbell	Conant
Bay City	Campbellton	Concord
Bayhill	Campville	Cone
Bay Port	Canaveral	Conway
Bay Ridge	Candler	Cork
Bay View	Cantonment	Cosmo
Beauclerc	Carlson	Cottondale
Belleview	Carrabelle	Cotton Plant
Bellville	Carterville	Courtney
Belmont	Caryville	Crandall
Belmore	Cason	Crawford
Benedict	Cassia	Crawfordville
Ben Haden	Castalia	Crescent City
Benton	Cedar Keys	Crestview
Beresford	Centre Hill	Crewsville
Berrydale	Centreville	Cromanton
Bethel	Cerro Gordo	Crown Point
Bilowry	Chaires	Crow's Bluff
Blackman	Charlotte Harbor	Crystal River
Blanton	Chaseville	Curtis Mills
Blitchton	Chattahoochee	Cutler
Bloomfield	Cherry Lake	Cypress
Bloomingdale	Chester	Dade City
Blount's Ferry	Chetwynd	Dallas
Blounstown	Chicora	Davenport
Bloxham	Chiefland	Daytona
Blue Spring	Chipco	DeFuniak Springs
Bluff Springs	Chipley	Dekle
Boardman	Chipola	DeLand
Bonifay	Chuluota	DeLeon Springs
Bostwick	Chumuckla	Dellwood
Boulogne	Churchill	Denaud
Bowling Green	Cincinnati	Denver
Bradfordville	Citra	Derby
Braiden Town	Citronelle	DeSota
Branford	City Point	Dinsmore
Brantley	Clarcona	Disston City
Bridge Creek	Clarksville	Dixon
Bridgeport	Clay Springs	Drayton Island
Bristol	Clear Water Harbor	Drifton
Bronson	Clermont	Duette
Brooksville	Cleveland	Duke
Broward	Clifton	Dunedin
Bryceville	Cocoa	Dunnellon
Buffalo Bluff	Cocoanut Grove	Dutton
Bushnell	Coe's Mills	Duval
Callahan	Coleman	Dyall
Calvinia	Columbia	Eagle Lake

Take the SAVANNAH, FLORIDA & WESTERN RAILWAY,
The Through Car and Short Line to and from Florida.

THE TROPICAL TRUNK LINE.

Jacksonville, Tampa and Key-West System

COVERS 1,000 MILES OF TROPICAL TERRITORY

EXTENDING SOUTHWARD FROM

Jacksonville, the Metropolis of Florida,

Through the Central portion of the Peninsula, and skirting both East and West Coasts, passing through Orange Groves, Fruit and Vegetable Farms, and is the only Line reaching to the

COCOANUT GROVES
—AND—
PINEAPPLE PLANTATIONS
OF THE
INDIAN RIVER AND LAKE WORTH COUNTRY

THE BEST EQUIPPED LINE IN THE SOUTH.

For Full Information, Maps, Schedules, Rates, etc., etc., address

G. D. ACKERLY, Gen'l Pass. Agent.

☞ Visit Green Cove Springs, a delightful Retreat for the Tourist, Invalid, Immigrant or Sportsman. Excellent Hotels, the Borden Parks, Fine Fishing and Hunting. Reached by Steamer or Train.

AND HER FAMOUS RESORTS. 103

Earleton	Forest City	Grover
Earnestville	Formosa	Guilford
Eastlake	Fort Drum	Gulf City
Eatonville	Fort Eagle	Gulf Hammock
Eau Gallie	Fort George	Hague
Econfina	Fort Green	Haines City
Eden	Fort McCoy	Halifax
Edwards	Fort Mason	Hamburg
Egleston	Fort Meade	Hamilton
Eldora	Fort Ogden	Hammock
Eldorado	Fort Pierce	Hampton
Eldridge	Fort Reed	Hardeeville
Electra	Fort White	Harmony
Ellaville	Foster Park	Harrison
Ellenton	Francis	Hart's Road
Ellerslie	Frankland	Harvard
Ellzey	Freeport	Harwood
Elmwood	Fruit Cove	Haskell
Emeralda	Fruitland	Hatch's Bend
Emerson	Fruitland Park	Hawk's Park
Emporia	Fulton	Hawthorn
Enos	Gabriella	Haywood's Landing
Enterprise	Gainsboro	Heath
Erie	Gainesville	Heidtville
Escambia	Geneva	Herlong
Estiffanulge	Georgetown	Hernando
Etoniah	Georgiana	Hibernia
Euchee Anna	Gilmore	Highland
Eureka	Glencoe	Highland Park
Eustis	Glendale	High Springs
Evergreen	Glen Ethel	Higley
Evinston	Glen St. Mary	Hilliard
Fairbanks	Glenwood	Hiwassee
Fairmount	Godwin	Hollister
Fairview	Gotha	Holly Hill
Fannin	Graceville	Holland
Fantville	Gracy	Holmes
Favorita	Grahamsville	Holt
Federal Hill	Grand Island	Homeland
Federal Point	Grand Ridge	Homosassa
Fellowship	Grasmere	Horsehead
Fernandina	Green Cove Springs	Horti
Ferry Pass	Greenland	Houston
Figulus	Green Pond	Hudnal
Flemington	Greenville	Hudson
Floral Bluff	Greenwood	Huntington
Floral City	Grove City	Hypoluxo
Florence	Grove Park	Iamonia

Take the SAVANNAH, FLORIDA & WESTERN RAILWAY,
The Through Car and Short Line to and from Florida.

HOTEL PLACIDE,

JACKSONVILLE, - - - - - - - **FLORIDA.**

ENTIRELY NEW.
CENTRALLY LOCATED.
AMERICAN AND EUROPEAN PLAN.
MOST ELABORATELY FURNISHED
AND
BEST EQUIPPED HOTEL IN THE CITY.

Passenger Elevator. Bells with Return Calls. Ample Fire Protection. Iron Fire Escapes. Fire Alarm in Every Room. Stationary Fire Hose on each Floor.

RATES, $3 to $4 PER DAY.

European Plan, $1 per Day and Upward.

LATEST STYLES. FINEST GOODS.

MRS. E. C. COFFIN,

Millinery, Dress Goods and Trimmings,

FANCY GOODS, FANS, LACES, GLOVES,

HOSIERY, UNDERWEAR.

57 West Bay Street, - JACKSONVILLE, FLA.

☞ Visit Green Cove Springs, a delightful Retreat for the Tourist, Invalid, Immigrant or Sportsman. Excellent Hotels, the Borden Parks. Fine Fishing and Hunting. Reached by Steamer or Train.

Iddo	Lake Maitland	Magdalene
Idlewild	Lake Mary	Magnolia Springs
Indianola	Lake Ogden	Malabar
Indian Springs	Lakeside	Malco
Inter Lachen	Lakeview	Manatee
Inwood	Lakeville	Mandarin
Iola	Lake Weir	Mango
Ionia	Lake Worth	Manfield
Island Grove	Lamont	Mannville
Island Lake	Lane Park	Marianna
Istachatta	Lanier	Marietta
Izagora	Lawtey	Marion
Jacksonville	Largo	Markham
Jasper	Lecanto	Marshville
Jennings	Lebanon	Martel
Jessamine	Lee	Martin
Jewell	Leesburg	Mary Esther
Johnson	Leitner	Marysville
John's Pass	Lenard	Mascotte
Jonesville	Leroy	Massacre
Judson	Lesly	Matanzas
Jupiter	Levyville	Maxville
Kanapaha	Limona	Mayo
Kathleen	Linden	Mayport
Keaton	Lisbon	Melbourne
Kendrick	Litesville	Melrose
Keuka	Little River	Merrifield
Keystone Park	Live Oak	Merrimack
Keysville	Liverpool	Merritt
Key West	Livingston	Messina
Killarney	Lloyd	Miakka
King's Ferry	Lochloosa	Miami
Kingsley	Lockwood	Micanopy
Kinney	Long Branch	Micco
Kissimmee	Long View	Miccosukee
Lacoochee	Longwood	Middleburgh
LaCrosse	Lowell	Midland
Lady Lake	Luraville	Midway
LaGrange	Lynne	Mikesville
Lake Bird	McAlpin	Miller's Ferry
Lake Butler	McCrab	Milligan
Lake City	McDavid	Millview
Lake Como	McIntosh	Milton
Lake Helen	McMeekin	Mims
Lake Howell	McRae	Minneola
Lake Joe	Macclenny	Molino
Lake Kerr	Macon	Montague
Lakeland	Madison	Montclair

Take the SAVANNAH, FLORIDA & WESTERN RAILWAY,
The Through Car and Short Line to and from Florida.

WHOLESALE AND RETAIL GROCERS.

HARKISHEIMER & CO.,
JACKSONVILLE, FLA.,

Agents for the Celebrated Roller Patent Victory Flour

AND

AVONDALE DAIRY BUTTER.

THE METROPOLIS.

THE PEOPLE'S PAPER.

DELIVERED TO ANY PART OF THE CITY AT

TEN CENTS A WEEK.

SPECIAL ADVERTISING ONE CENT A WORD.

Complete Local News, with State and General News,

CARTER & RUSSELL, Proprietors.

J. W. WHITE'S
ADVERTISING AGENCY

JACKSONVILLE, - FLORIDA.

EVERYTHING IN THE ADVERTISING LINE DONE PROMPTLY

HIGHEST REFERENCES.

YEARS OF EXPERIENCE.

☞ Visit Green Cove Springs, a delightful Retreat for the Tourist, Invalid, Immigrant or Sportsman. Excellent Hotels, the Borden Parks, Fine Fishing and Hunting. Reached by Steamer or Train.

Monte Vista
Monticello
Morganville
Montverde
Moseley Hall
Moss Bluff
Mossy Head
Moultrie
Mount Dora
Mounteocha
Mount Pleasant
Mount Tabor
Myers
Naples
Narcoossee
Narrows
Nashua
Natural Bridge
Neal's Landing
Nesbitt
New Augustine
New Berlin
New Cadiz
Newnansville
New Smyrna
New Troy
Nocatee
Norwalk
Norway
Oakdale
Oak Grove
Oak Hill
Oakland
Oak Lawn
Oak Villa
Obrine Station
Ocala
Ocklawaha
Ocklocknee
Ocoee
Octahatchee
Okahumpka
Old Town
Olive
Olustee
Oneco
Orange
Orange Bend

Orange City
Orange Dale
Orange Heights
Orange Hill
Orange Home
Orange Lake
Orange Mills
Orange Park
Orange Springs
Orchid
Oriole
Orlando
Orleans
Ormond
Osceola
Osprey
Osteen
Otahite
Otter Creek
Oviedo
Owens
Owensboro
Oxford
Ozona
Pablo Beach
Padlock
Paisley
Palatka
Palma Sola
Palm Beach
Palmer
Palmetto
Palm Springs
Panama Park
Panasoffkee
Paola
Paradise
Parish
Parker
Parkersburgh
Pasadena
Pelot
Pemberton
Penial
Penn
Pensacola
Peoria
Perry

Peru
Pettway
Philps
Picolata
Picnic
Pierson
Pine Barren
Pine Castle
Pine Level
Pinellas
Pinemount
Pinhook
Pittnam
Plant City
Plymouth
Point Washington
Pomona
Ponce de Leon
Ponce Park
Portland
Port Orange
Port Richey
Providence
Punta Gorda
Punta Rassa
Putnam Hall
Quincy
Racy Point
Raulerson
Red Bay
Reddick
Rhodes Store
Richland
Ridgewood
River Junction
Riverside
Rixford
Roberts
Rochelle
Rock Bluff
Rock Ledge
Rock Springs
Romeo
Rosehill
Rosewood
Rural
Rutland
Rutledge

Take the SAVANNAH, FLORIDA & WESTERN RAILWAY,
The Through Car and Short Line to and from Florida.

The Place to Buy your Men's, Boys' and Children's Clothing, Gents' Furnishing Goods and Hats.

G. HESS,

11 WEST BAY ST., - JACKSONVILLE, FLA.

FINE GOODS AT POPULAR PRICES.

WE CARRY THE LARGEST STOCK OF FINE

TAILOR MADE CLOTHING

In the State, and guarantee to you a better made up garment than any of our competitors for a great deal less money. Call and examine

Our Large and Elegant Stock.

All goods guaranteed as represented or money cheerfully refunded. We invite inspection.

G. HESS,

THE LARGEST CLOTHIER AT POPULAR PRICES IN THE STATE.

11 West Bay Street, Jacksonville, Fla.

☞ Visit Green Cove Springs, a delightful Retreat for the Tourist, Invalid, Immigrant or Sportsman. Excellent Hotels, the Borden Parks, Fine Fishing and Hunting. Reached by Rail or Steamer.

Rye	Sparr	Verona
Saint Andrew's Bay	Spring Garden	Viana
Saint Augustine	Spring Grove	Victoria
Saint Cloud	Spring Warrior	Villa City
Saint Francis	Stage Pond	Viola
Saint James City	Stanton	Wahneta
Saint Lucie	Starke	Wakulla
Saint Marks	Steinhatchee	Waldo
Saint Nicholas	Stephensville	Wauchula
Saint Petersburg	Sterling	Warrington
Saint Teresa	Stockton	Waukeenah
Saint Thomas	Stonewall	Waveland
Salem	Sumner	Waylonzo
San Antonia	Summerfield	Webster
Sanderson	Summerlin	Weir Park
Sandy	Summit	Wekiva
Sanford	Sumterville	Welaka
Sanibel	Sunny Hill	Wellborn
San Mateo	Sunnyside	Welshton
San Pablo	Sutherland	West Apopka
Santa Rosa Park	Suwannee	Westfarm
Santos	Suwannee Shoals	Westville
Sarasota	Switzerland	Wetappo
Satsuma	Sycamore	Wetumpka
Satsuma Hights	Sylvan Lake	Wewahitchka
Sauble	Syracuse	White Springs
Scotland	Tallahassee	Whitney
Seaside	Tampa	Wilderness
Sebastian	Tangerine	Wildwood
Seffner	Tarpon Springs	Williston
Seller's Lake	Tavares	Willow
Selman	Temple's Mills	Windermere
Seminole	Thompson	Windsor
Seneca	Thonotosassa	Winnemissett
Seville	Tillman	Winsted
Sharon	Titusville	Winter Haven
Shell Creek	Tocoi	Winter Park
Shiloh	Tompkinsville	Wiscon
Silver Pond	Trenton	Woodbridge
Silver Springs	Tropic	Woodville
Silver Springs Park	Turnbull	Worthington
Sisco	Twin Lakes	Wyoma
Smith Creek	Tyner	Yallaha
Sneads	Umatilla	Youmans
Sopchoppy	Underhill	Zellwood
Sorrento	Union	Zif
South Jacksonville	Venice	Zion
South Lake Weir	Vernon	Zolfo

Take the SAVANNAH, FLORIDA & WESTERN RAILWAY,
The Through Car and Short Line to and from Florida.

ESTABLISHED FROM JANUARY TO OCTOBER, 1890.

Alliance	Harbor View	Port Tampa
Avoca	Harlem	Potolo
Baywood	Hartland	President City
Brandon	Hermitage	Raymond
Brent	Hoskins	Riverland
Brooklyn	Idalia	Safety Harbor
Broughton	Imri	Sampala
Buckingham	Ivanhoe	Sharpes
Buda	Jensen	Sim's City
Coquina	Lake Ashby	Spring Lake
Cora	Lesley	Stewartville
Dahoma	Limestone	Tahiti
Disston City	Magnolia Springs	Theressa
Ealum	Melvin	Upsala
Ehren	Motto	Valkaria
Ethel	Newport	Watertown
Farmdale	Norvella	Winfield
Fidelis	Ocheesee	Withlacoochee
Gaiter	Palermo	Wood
Garfield	Patterson	York
Genoa	Pineaway	Yular
Hagen	Plummers	

TRANSPORTATION LINES.

RAILROADS.

Atlantic and Western Railway—From Orange City to Lake Helen and New Smyrna. Connects with Jacksonville, Tampa and Key West Railway.

Florida Midland Railway—From Longwood to Windermere. Connects with the South Florida Railroad at Longwood, and the Tavares, Orlando and Atlantic Railroad at Apopka.

Florida Central and Peninsular Railroad—From Jacksonville to all points West and Southwest. Western Division—New Orleans, Tallahassee and Jacksonville. Southern Division—Fernandina and Jacksonville to Orlando. Tampa Branch—Wildwood to Plant City. Fernandina and Jacksonville Division—Jacksonville to Fernandina. St. Marks Division—From Tallahassee to St. Marks. Cedar Key Division—From Waldo to Cedar Key.

Florida Southern Railway (J., T. & K. W. System)—From Palatka to Brooksville. St. Johns and Eustis Division—From Leesburg to Astor. Charlotte Harbor Division—From Bartow to Punta Gorda.

☞ **Visit Green Cove Springs, a delightful Retreat for the Tourist, Invalid, Immigrant or Sportsman. Excellent Hotels, the Borden Parks, Fine Fishing and Hunting. Reached by Steamer or Train.**

Jacksonville and Atlantic Railroad—From Jacksonville to Pablo Beach.

Georgia Southern and Florida—From Palatka to Macon, Ga., via Lake City, connecting with the F. C. & P. Railway.

Jacksonville, Mayport, Pablo Railway and Navigation Company—From Jacksonville to Mayport and Burnside Beach.

Jacksonville, Tampa and Key West Railway—From Jacksonville to Titusville and Tavares.

Jacksonville, St. Augustine and Halifax River Railway—From Jacksonville to St Augustine. From St. Augustine to Palatka and Daytona. From St. Augustine to Tocoi.

Jupiter and Lake Worth Railway—From Jupiter to Juno, on Lake Worth.

Louisville and Nashville Railway (Pensacola Division)—From Jacksonville to New Orleans, via Pensacola.

Orange Belt Railway—From Sanford to St. Petersburg.

Pensacola and Perdido Railroad—From Pensacola to Millview.

South Florida Railroad (Main Line)—From Sanford to Tampa and Port Tampa. Bartow Branch—From Bartow Junction to Bartow. Pemberton Ferry Branch—From Bartow to Pemberton Ferry. Indian River Division—Sanford to Lake Charm.

Silver Spring, Ocala and Gulf Railroad—From Ocala to Homosassa and Crystal River.

Sugar Belt Railroad—From Kissimmee to St. Cloud.

Tavares, Apopka and Gulf Railroad—From Tavares to Clermont.

Tavares, Orlando and Atlantic Railroad—From Orlando to Tavares.

Waycross Short Line—From Jacksonville to all points.

STEAMSHIP LINES.

Clyde's New York, Charleston and Florida Steamship Company—From Jacksonville to New York.

Mallory Steamship Company—From Fernandina to New York.

Ocean Steamship Company—From Florida to Philadelphia, New York and Boston

Plant Steamship Company—From Tampa to Havana.

Southern Pacific Company's Steamers—Between New Orleans, Charlotte Harbor, Key West and Havana.

Tampa Steamship Company—From Tampa to Mobile.

STEAMBOAT LINES.

Beach & Miller Line Steamers—From Jacksonville to Fort George, Orange Park, Green Cove Springs, Palatka and Lake George.

Clyde's St. Johns River—From Jacksonville to Sanford and intermediate points.

Hart's Ocklawaha Line—From Palatka to Silver Spring and intermediate points.

Take the SAVANNAH, FLORIDA & WESTERN RAILWAY,
The Through Car and Short Line to and from Florida.

Steamer Farmer—From Fernandina to Savannah.
Indian River Steamboat Company—From Titusville to Jupiter.
Steamer City of Brunswick—From Fernandina to Brunswick.
Steamer Martha—Fernandina and St. Marys River.
Kissimmee and Nacoosee Steamboat Company—From Kissimmee to Nacoosee and Fort Bassenger.
Post Day Line—Jacksonville to Palatka.
Steamer from Jacksonville to Fort George.
Steamer Manatee—From Jacksonville to Mandarin and Green Cove Springs.
Steamer A. J. Lane—Eustis and Lake Harris.
Steamer Alice Howard—St. James on-the-Gulf and Fort Myers.
Steamer Rockledge—Indian River Line.
Steamer Edith—Palatka to Picolata.
Steamer Kissimmee—From Port Tampa to Manatee River points.

FLORIDA SUB-TROPICAL EXPOSITION—OPENS JANUARY, 1891—FOURTH SEASON.

☞ Visit Green Cove Springs, a delightful Retreat for the Tourist, Invalid, Immigrant or Sportsman. Excellent Hotels, the Borden Parks, Fine Fishing and Hunting. Reached by Steamer or Train.

www.ingramcontent.com/pod-product-compliance
Lightning Source LLC
Chambersburg PA
CBHW031404160426
43196CB00007B/885